拼盤與盤飾

Chinese Appetizers
& Garnishes

Author:	Huang Su-Huei 黃淑惠
Translator:	Chen Chang-Yen 陳常彥
Collaborator:	Gloria C. Martinez
Publisher:	Huang Su-Huei 黃淑惠
Platters prepared by:	Wei-Chuan's Cooking
	Full Sun Restaurant 福陞川菜館
	Ting Tzu-Ping 丁自平
	Lee Mu-Tsun 李木村
	Wu Tzu-Chiang 吳志強
	Wu Sen-Chuan 吳森泉
	Chang Shui-Thu 張水土
	Wen Shang-Hsing 溫上興
	Yeh Jia-Tzu 葉佳祖
	Cheng Ah-Fu 鄭阿福
	Lay Biau 賴標
	Shiao Fa-Tsai 蕭發財
Photographer:	Aki Ohno
	T. S. Wang 王鐵石
	Lin Kun Hon 林坤鴻
Designer:	Ken Fukuda
	Shaw, Haizan 蕭多皆
Typesetting:	Alton Litho Printers
Printed by:	China Color Printing Co., Inc.

ISBN 0-941676-01-3

序

　　本公司繼中國菜及中國餐點後，在民國六十九年七月又出版了一本中國菜第二册，是由葉澄惠女士主編，其內容略有創新，除了食譜外更包括了一些餐盤裝飾，出書以來引起國內外讀者的熱烈反應，均表示對餐盤裝飾的興趣和喜愛。

　　我們有感於中國菜第二册所包括的盤飾內容有限，恐不能滿足愛好者的需要，因此，我們決定由各方面再收集更多更完善的資料編寫成這本專門性的書籍—"拼盤與盤飾"來介紹中國烹飪藝術的更高境界。

　　茲將此書之內容簡介如後：

1. 拼盤與盤飾按其形式，用場及取材來分類介紹。

2. 切雕之方法除有文字說明外並有圖片配合，使讀者極易明瞭。

3. 內容包括有製作非常簡易的，也有較複雜的，個人可視其需要來選擇學習的項目。

4. 本書同時也收集了一些較具特色的拼盤和盤飾，可配合節慶或喜宴使用。

　　拼盤和盤飾在烹飪上是屬於特殊技巧的部份，需要有純熟的手藝和靈巧的心思，才能有新的多變化的作品。當然也需要適當的工具來配合，在本書製作時曾請多位專家協助，他們所使用的工具也不盡相同，均視其個人的習慣和方便來選擇。不過，除了少數較特殊的盤飾需要用特製的雕花刀外，通常　用薄菜刀和小尖刀即能做出各類盤飾，在文中另有專欄介紹工具，故不贅敍。

　　為製作本書我們曾多方收集了許多資料，但考慮到篇幅有限，故僅就所需精選了部份，在製作當中我們深深感覺到烹飪的切雕藝術的確非常有趣，其中之千變萬化全在於製作者的巧妙運用。我希望讀者能本著參考研究的心情來學習這項技術，更希望您能運用巧思推陳出新，創作出您自己的傑作。又本書內容如有疏誤之處，敬請讀者們不吝指正。

Introduction

In July of 1980 we published CHINESE CUISINE II, compiled by Ms. Yeh Cheng-Huei. This book differed from my other cookbooks, CHINESE CUISINE, CHINESE SNACKS, and CHINESE COOKING For Beginners, because it included a section on the preparation of garnishes. The public response to CHINESE CUISINE II, locally and from abroad, was very gratifying and encouraging to me—I am very grateful for this. The great interest in the preparation of garnishes encouraged me to consult many experts in this field and to gather much information about garnishes. In an effort to present the public with more and varied garnishes, I am pleased that we are now able to introduce this specialty book on the artistic level of Chinese cookery—CHINESE APPETIZERS AND GARNISHES. It includes:

1. Appetizers and garnishes that are presented according to difficulty, ingredients, and occasions they are usually served.
2. Various methods of carving that are clearly explained and can be easily followed by looking at the smaller "hands on" photographs.
3. Procedures that range in difficulty from simple to complex. The wide variety allows the selection of the particular appetizers and garnishes to suit the individual needs.
4. A collection of special appetizers and garnishes that may be used for special occasions.

Appetizers and garnishes require particular techniques to prepare. The artistic carving techniques belong to a special class in the art of serving Chinese cuisine. The carving techniques take practice to acquire; however, once the techniques have been acquired, any creative design may be made. Suitable cutting utensils are necessary. The utensils and carving tools used by the experts differed with individual preference. A thin-blade cleaver and a sharp pointed knife were used to prepare most of the garnishes. Only the intricate designs and special garnishes required the use of the special carving tools. The names of the carving tools used for the special garnishes are listed in another section of this book.

The collection of garnishes and appetizers for this book is extensive. A select few were chosen for this edition. We found the art of carving and preparing garnishes to be very interesting and that it could be adapted by the maker, depending upon the facility in the use of the tools and the creative ability of each person.

The purpose of this book is to serve as a reference book. I hope the readers will be inspired to do more research on their own to learn more about this art form. In addition, I hope that after the basic techniques are learned, the reader will create individual designs and develop new carving techniques.

It has been my practice to listen to and to consider suggestions, recommendations, and contributions that readers have made regarding my books. In an effort to provide a practical and beautiful book on Chinese cookery, I plan to continue this practice with my book on CHINESE APPETIZERS AND GARNISHES.

Huang Su-Huei

Huang Su-Huei

目錄・TABLE OF CONTENTS

餐盤裝飾 • GARNISHES

實用型
Adaptable Garnishes

番 茄 類	Tomato	1-3
蘿 蔔 類	White Radish and Carrot	4
黃 瓜 類	Cucumber	5
小紅蘿蔔類	Radish	7
小 花 類	Small Flower	9
葱、蘋果、檸檬類	Scallion, Apple and Lemon	11

特殊型
Special Garnishes

麵 條 花 籃	Noodle Basket	13
番 茄 花 籃	Tomato Basket	15
蘿 蔔 花	White Radish Flower	17
花 樹	Flower Tree	19
魚 網	Fish Net	21
金 魚	Goldfish	23
瓜 盅	Winter Squash	25
天 鵝	Two Graceful Swans	27
雞 群	Spring Is Everywhere	57

拼盤 • APPETIZERS

基本型
Basic Appetizers

大 拼	Variety Appetizer Platter	29
單 拼	One-ingredient Appetizer	29
雙 拼	Two-ingredients Appetizer	29
三 色 拼 盤	Three-ingredients Appetizer	29

一般型
Popular Appetizers

柒 星 轉 盤	Seven-colors Lazy Susan	31
五 彩 轉 盤	Five-flavors Lazy Susan	31
柒 味 大 拼	Seven-flavors Star	33
五 福 拼 盤	Five-flavors Plum Blossom	33
一 品 拼 盤	Circles of Delight Platter	35
錦 繡 拼 盤	Circles of Grandeur Platter	35
梅 花 蝦 片	Plum Blossom Shrimp Platter	37
壽 桃 蝦 片	Long-life Shrimp Platter	37

四色拼盤
Assorted Appetizers

壽 字 腰 花	Long-life Kidney Platter	39
五 香 牛 肉	Sliced Five-spice Roast Beef	39
滷 鴨	Duck Flavored with Soy Sauce	39
鹽 水 肫 肝	Sliced Gizzards Platter	39
餚 肉	Tasty Chinese Ham Slices	41
棒 棒 雞	Shredded Chicken Platter	41
蜇 皮 捲	Chinese Cabbage Rolls	41
五 香 牛 肉	Sliced Five-spice Roast Beef	41
酥 炸 鳳 尾 魚	Deep-fried Fish Platter	43
滷 鴨 舌	Duck Tongues Flavored with Soy Sauce	43
紅 燒 冬 菇	Chinese Black Mushrooms Dish	43

銀芽鮑魚絲 Shredded Abalone and Bean Sprouts 43

大宴拼盤
**Elegant Appetizer
Platters**

鳳 鳥 來 儀 The Arrival of the Phoenix 45
祥 龍 獻 瑞 The Good Luck Dragon 47
孔 雀 開 屏 The Proud Peacock 49
梅 花 拼 盤 Winter Plum Flower 51
松 鶴 延 年 Two Graceful Symbols of Longevity 53
花 籃 拼 盤 A Basket of Spring Flowers 55
錦 繡 雀 屏 The Colorful Peacock 57
龍 舟 競 渡 The Dragon Yacht Race 59
藍 橋 相 會 Meeting at Blue Bridge 61
永 矢 同 心 Lend a Note of Love and Unity 63
一 帆 風 順 Bon Voyage 63
龍 柱 呈 祥 The Dragon Pillar 63
彩 蝶 飛 Two Butterflies 65

做法詳解 ● HOW TO MAKE APPETIZERS AND GARNISHES

蘋 菓 盤 飾 Apple Garnish 66
番 茄 盤 飾 Tomato Garnishes 67-75
茄 子 盤 飾 Chinese Eggplant Garnishes 76-78
辣 椒 盤 飾 Red Pepper Garnishes 79-80
蒜 類 盤 飾 Fresh Garlic Garnish 81
葱 類 盤 飾 Scallion Garnish 82
洋 葱 盤 飾 Brown Onion Garnish 83
黃 瓜 盤 飾 Cucumber Garnishes 84-90
胡 瓜 盤 飾 Vegetable Marrow Garnish 91
冬 瓜 盤 飾 Winter Squash Garnishes 92-93
芋 頭 盤 飾 Taro Root Garnish 94
白蘿蔔盤飾 White Radish Garnishes 95-108
紅蘿蔔盤飾 Carrot Garnishes 109-120
小紅蘿蔔盤飾 Radish Garnishes 121-124
菜 莖 盤 飾 Vegetable Stem Garnishes 125-126
合 拼 盤 飾 Variety Garnishes 127-140
雞 肉 盤 飾 Chicken Meat Platters 141-142
牛 肉 盤 飾 Cold Beef Platter 143
腰 子 盤 飾 Kidney Garnishes 144-146
皮 蛋 盤 飾 One Thousand Year Egg Platter 147
蛋 黃 盤 飾 Egg Yolk Garnish 148
麵 條 盤 飾 Noodle Basket Garnish 149
木須肉皮盤飾 Moo Shu Skin (Wrapper) Garnish 150
馬鈴薯盤飾 Potato Garnish 151

KNIVES AND CARVING TOOLS
USED TO PREPARE GARNISHES

做盤飾之工具並無一定之規格，端視個人之習慣和使用的方便來
選擇。一般的盤飾通常僅用薄菜刀和尖刀就可做，但
有一些較特殊的盤飾則需用特製的雕花刀來做。
此外，剪刀也算是做盤飾的工具之一。
茲將本書中所使用的工具分別說明如下：

The carving tools used to prepare the garnishes may be
slightly different from those in the illustration. Most of
the garnishes can be made with a thin-blade cleaver and a sharp-pointed knife;
however, some garnishes do require the use of special carving tools. In
addition, a pair of scissors is also used to prepare garnishes.
The following guide explains all the knives and carving tools used to prepare the
garnishes presented in this book.

薄 菜 刀：
Thin-Blade Cleaver

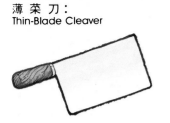

舉凡切塊、切片等均使用薄菜刀。

The thin-blade cleaver is used to slice and cut material into sections.

尖 刀：
Sharp-Pointed Knife

用來雕較細膩的部份，例如：雕花瓣、片薄皮、刻鋸齒花紋等。

The sharp-pointed knife is used to make fine and delicate cuts, such as, carving petals, slicing the skin of a vegetable, or cutting v-shaped grooves.

剪 刀：
Scissors

通常都是用來剪花瓣，如：辣椒花、葱花及紅蘿蔔花等。

A pair of scissors is used to cut the red pepper petals, the green onion flowers and the carrot petals.

尖形雕刀：
V-Shaped-Blade Carving Tool

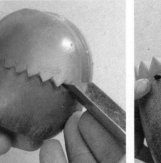

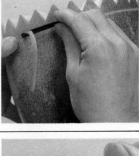

適合用來雕尖形花瓣、刻鋸齒紋、劃線條等。

The v-shaped-blade carving tool is used to make pointed petals, v-shaped grooves, and strips.

圓形雕刀：
Curved-Blade Carving Tool

適合用來雕圓形花瓣，或挖圓孔。

The curved-blade carving tool is used to make the scallop petals.

雕花刀本公司有售　Knives and carving tools are sold in our company.

A

B

C

D

番 茄 類

番茄盤飾是最實用的盤飾之一，用不同的蔬菜來襯托，可產生多種變化。

A. 番茄切兩半，再分別切刻後與黃瓜一同擺飾於盤旁，十分美觀。番茄做法參考第69頁。黃瓜做法參考第133頁，切二片相連的薄片，將其中一片內摺，交錯排列即成。

B. 用番茄刻花來取代鴨頭或雞頭的位置。番茄做法參考第66頁。黃瓜做法參考第89頁。

C. 用番茄做成花籃，可用來裝醬汁，亦可當盤飾，做法參考74頁。黃瓜做法參考第85頁。

D. 大圓盤外圈以生菜絲墊底，其上排以7─8瓣番茄，此種盤飾可用於宴席上的大菜。番茄做法參考第67頁。

GARNISHES—
ADAPTABLE GARNISHES

Tomato

The tomato garnish is one of the most useful garnishes. It can be embellished with different kinds of vegetables and carved to produce a variety of designs.

A. The "stepladder-like" tomato garnish adds color and elegance to this platter of rolls of "good fortune". For directions to make the tomato garnish see p. 69. Directions for the delicate cucumber garnish may be found on p. 133, with the exception that only two slices are joined; bend one slice toward the joined end. Arrange the cucumber slices alternately one side then the other side.

B. Use the tomato skin rose garnish to serve as the head of the chicken or duck. See p. 66 for directions to make this tomato garnish. Directions for the cucumber garnish may be found on p. 89.

C. A tomato basket can be used to hold a sauce or as a garnish. See p. 74 for directions to make the tomato basket and p. 85 for directions to make the cucumber garnish.

D. Rest the simple tomato garnish wedges around a bed of shredded lettuce to encircle the shrimp balls. This garnish can be used for banquets. Directions for this garnish may be found on p. 67.

E

F

G

H

I

J

2

番 茄 類

E. 僅用兩瓣番茄將皮片開相對擺飾，再配些生菜絲及香菜，可當配料亦可當盤飾。

F. 少許白蘿蔔絲墊底，擺上番茄花，並以巴西利點綴。番茄做法參考第73頁。

G. 番茄切半後再切片，排於盤邊，可當配料亦可當盤飾。

H. 將生菜切絲墊底，黃瓜當葉，中間飾以番茄花。黃瓜做法參考第86頁。番茄做法參考第66頁。

I. 取少許芹菜葉墊底，上置番茄花。番茄做法參考第66頁。

J. 紅色番茄配以幾片香菜葉，簡單而美觀。番茄做法參考第71頁。

GARNISHES— ADAPTABLE GARNISHES

Tomato

E. Use two tomato wedges for this garnish. Remove the skin from the meat. Place the two wedges in opposite directions. The tomato wedges can be used as part of the salad or as a garnish.

F. Place the tomato skin rose garnish on a bed of shredded white radish. Tuck in a parsley sprig on one side of the rose. See p. 73 for directions to make the tomato garnish.

G. Cut a tomato in half; then slice each half into thin slices. Arrange the tomato slices around the plate by overlapping them. The tomato slices may be included as one of the ingredients or as a garnish.

H. This shallow tomato skin rose rests on a bed of shredded lettuce. See p. 66 for directions to make the tomato garnish. Arrange the cucumber garnishes, that will serve as leaves; then place the tomato garnish in the center. See p. 86 for directions to make the cucumber garnish.

I. Place some celery leaves on the side of the serving platter; then place the tomato skin flower on top of the celery leaves. See p. 66 for directions to make this tomato garnish.

J. This simple but beautiful tomato garnish, with its diamond-shaped center, complements any dish; the Chinese parsley (cilantro), on both sides, adds delicate and graceful lines. See p. 71 for directions to make this garnish.

3

A

B

餐盤裝飾— 實用型

蘿 蔔 類

A.**B**.**C**.圖所示的三種盤飾，均採用經濟實惠的材料，可選購中或小型的紅或白蘿蔔來做。

A 圖做法參考第 132 頁。
B 圖做法參考第 130 頁。
C 圖做法參考第 95 頁。

GARNISHES— ADAPTABLE GARNISHES

White Radish and Carrot

The garnishes in Pictures A, B, and C are made with economical ingredients. Select a small or medium white radish or carrot for these garnishes. The directions to make these garnishes may be found on the following pages:

A carrot garnish, page 132;
B carrot garnish, page 130;
C white radish garnish, page 95.

C

A

B

C

餐盤裝飾—實用型

黃 瓜 類

A. 在帶點清湯的菜餚邊，放置四個黃瓜盤飾，清爽而美觀。黃瓜做法參考第85頁。

B. 黃瓜斜切薄片，一邊相連不切斷，圍排在盤邊，可當配料亦可當盤飾。

C. 黃瓜做法參考第114頁的紅蘿蔔盤飾6，表面不刻任何花紋，修成薄片後將兩端向內捲成喇叭狀。雀巢做法參考第151頁。

GARNISHES— ADAPTABLE GARNISHES

Cucumber

A. Four cucumber garnishes are placed around this dish to serve as a simple but beautiful garnish. See p. 85 for directions to make the cucumber garnish.

B. Diagonally slice the cucumbers, do not cut through; fan out the slices then arrange them around the dish by overlapping them. The garnish may be eaten as part of the prepared dish.

C. See p. 114, Carrot Garnish 6, for directions to make the cucumber garnish; however, do not carve a design on the skin of the cucumber. Cut the cucumber into a thin spiral slice (curl); bend the two ends in toward the center. See p. 151 for directions to make the bird's nest.

A

C

B

D

6

小紅蘿蔔類

小紅蘿蔔內白外紅，除色澤美觀外，亦容易
切刻，故很適合做盤飾之材料。

A 圖盤飾做法參考第122頁。
B 圖盤飾做法參考第91頁的胡瓜盤飾圖②、圖③。
C 圖盤飾做法參考第 124 頁及 129 頁。
D 圖盤飾做法參考第 123 頁。

GARNISHES—
ADAPTABLE GARNISHES

Radish Garnish

The radish is a very good vegetable to use as a garnish. The red radish with its white inside may be carved in a variety of ways to accent the color of any dish.

Directions to make these garnishes may be found on the following pages:

A page 122;
B page 91, Vegetable Marrow Garnish, Figures ②-③;
C pages 124 and 129;
D page 123.

A

B

C

D

E

F

8

小 花 類

這類小花做法簡易可任意取材，如白蘿蔔、紅蘿蔔、小紅蘿蔔、黃瓜、茄子等。使用時可單獨一朵擺飾，或數朵花插在花籃內，擺於盤中或盤邊，非常實用。

小花做法參考第 129 頁。
B 圖花籃做法參考第 102 頁。
D 圖葱花做法參考第81頁。
F 圖菜莖做法參考第 125 頁。

GARNISHES— ADATABLE GARNISHES

Small Flowers

This kind of small flowers are practical and easy to make. Select any vegetable such as white radish, carrot radish, cucumber, eggplant, etc. One flower can be used as the center of the garnish or it can be arranged with several flowers in the center or side of the platter.

Direction to make these flowers are found on the following pages:
small flowers, page 129;
B basket garnish, page 102;
D scallion garnish, page 81;
F vegetable stem garnish, page 125.

A

B

C

D

10

蔥、蘋果、檸檬 類

A. 菜餚是金黃色，以白色蔥花相襯，特別出色。蔥花做法參考第82頁。

B. 使用蘋果做盤飾，色澤艷麗，非常別緻。做法參考第69頁。

C. 蘋果花做法參考第66頁

D. 暗色的菜餚配以紅、黃二色的盤飾，顯得明朗而出色。檸檬做法參考第66頁。黃瓜做法參考第89頁。

GARNISHES— ADAPTABLE GARNISHES

Scallion, Apple and Lemon

A. This golden-color shrimp dish is decorated with a white scallion garnish. The garnish adds color and beauty. See p. 82 for directions to make the scallion garnish.

B. Use an apple for this garnish, the color is beautiful and the design is special. See p. 69 for directions to make this garnish.

C. This delicate red-tipped rose adds elegance to this platter. See p. 66 for directions to make the apple garnish.

D. Brighten up this dish with red and yellow garnishes. See p. 66 for directions to make the lemon and tomato garnishes and p. 89 for directions to make the cucumber garnish.

麵條花籃

麵條做的花籃有數種，此爲簡易的一種。可
任選菜餚裝入籃中，籃下也可隨意排些盤飾
。花籃做法參考第 149 頁。

GARNISHES— SPECIAL GARNISHES

Noodle Basket

There are many different kinds of noodle baskets. Here we introduce you to an easy kind. You can place food in the basket and arrange some colorful garnishes on the plate. See page 149 for the directions to make this noodle basket.

蘿 蔔 花

鮮紅色的螃蟹置於嫩綠生菜葉上，並配以黃
、紅、綠色的盤飾，分外耀眼。蘿蔔花做法
參考第99頁。番茄做法參考第69頁。

GARNISHES— SPECIAL GARNISHES
White Radish Flowers

Place the cooked crab on top of a bed
of green lettuce leaves. Decorate the
platter with yellow, red, and green
garnishes to add different colors. See
page 99 for directions to make the bright
pink white radish flower. Directions to
make the tomato garnish may be found
on page 69.

花　　樹

將菜餚圍排在大盤四週，中央置一塊白蘿蔔，上插西洋芹菜莖當花枝，再插上一些小花。或再用蘿蔔刻壽桃圖案擺飾盤邊，即可用在慶壽酒宴上。小花做法參考第114頁，蘿蔔表面不刻任何花紋，修成四方柱再將一端修尖成錐形，片薄片後捲成花朵。

GARNISHES— SPECIAL GARNISHES

Flower Tree

Arrange the squabs around the platter. Place a piece of white radish in the center. Insert a celery stick in the center of the white radish; then insert some small flowers in the celery branches. OR, Use white radish to carve out some "long life" designs and place them on the side of the platter for decoration. This dish can be used for birthday celebrations. See p. 114 for directions to make the small flowers; however, do not carve a design on the skin of the white radish (or carrot). Cut the white radish to a rectangular shape; trim one end to a point. At the pointed end, thinly slice in a circular fashion to obtain a "curl". Roll the slice of white radish to form a flower.

餐盤裝飾─特殊型

魚　網

此種魚網做起來較費時，但一條紅蘿蔔即可
做成一大張魚網，非常有趣。

魚網做法參考第 120 頁
番茄做法參考第69頁
黃瓜做法參考第84頁及85頁

GARNISHES──
SPECIAL GARNISHES

Fish Net

This garnish may require more time,
patience, and concentration to make
than the other garnishes, but it is
fascinating to see how a long, thin slice
of carrot is transformed into a big net. The
directions to make these garnishes may
be found on the following pages; fish
net, page 120; tomato garnish, page 69;
cucumbers, pages 84 and 85.

餐盤裝飾─特殊型

金　魚

這種盤飾與前面所介紹的盤飾略不同，使用多種材料組成金魚形狀，用來做菜餚或盤飾均可。做法參考第 136 頁。

GARNISHES— SPECIAL GARNISHES

Goldfish

This garnish is different from the other garnishes because several kinds of ingredients are required to make a fish figure. It can be included as an ingredient in a dish or used as a garnish. See page 136 for directions to make this goldfish garnish.

瓜盅

這種瓜盅除了瓜肉可食之外，瓜皮上還雕有精細的圖案，同時亦具備了盤飾的效果。雕法參考第92頁和93頁，僅將圖案改變。盤邊所圍之如意捲可當為配料也可做盤飾。其做法是，煎好的蛋皮上塗一層蝦絨，鋪上一張紫菜，再塗一層蝦絨，由兩端分別往中央捲起，蒸熟後切片使用。

GARNISHES— SPECIAL GARNISHES

Winter Squash

This winter squash has a beautiful design carved on the skin. The meat of the squash may be served as a vegetable; the design carved on the skin serves as a garnish. See pages 92 and 93 for directions to carve a design or to create an original design. The good fortune rolls around the platter can be used as part of the prepared dish or as a garnish. To make the good fortune rolls: first make the eggroll skins (wrappers); then spread the shrimp paste on the skin. Next, place a sheet of nori (seaweed) on the skin; additional ingredients may be placed on the nori. Again, spread some shrimp paste on the nori. Roll the layered wrapper tightly from both ends in toward the center. Steam the good fortune rolls until cooked; remove. Cut them into thick slices.

天　鵝

此種盤飾在比較特殊的場合才使用。需選擇較大的白蘿蔔來做，雕刻所費時間亦較長，雕出的天鵝必須生動自然才能配合用場。做法參考第 107 頁。

GARNISHES— SPECIAL GARNISHES

Two Graceful Swans

These two beautiful and graceful swans are enjoying a leisurely swim in a pool of love. Their closeness depicts the closeness of two lovers. This beautiful arrangement is used for festive occasions and to celebrate newlyweds. The large bowl at the bottom is used as a tureen for soup of individual preference. The smaller bowl is used to hold the lovely pair of swans. See page 107 for dirctions to make the swans.

拼盤—基本型

拼盤排放時需注意先後順序，茲例舉下列四種供參考。

大　拼A
做法參考第 139 頁

單　拼B
做法參考第 137 頁

雙　拼C
做法參考第 138 頁

三色拼盤D
做法與雙拼相似，僅中間再多放一項材料即可。

D

APPETIZERS—
BASIC APPETIZERS

When arranging the appetizer platters, special attention must be given to the order in which the ingredients are placed. Below are four basic appetizers:

Variety Appetizer Platter A
To arrange the platter, see p. 139.

One-ingredient Appetizer B
To arrange the platter, see p. 137.

Two-ingredients Appetizer C
To arrange the platter, see p. 138.

Three-ingredients Appetizer D
This platter is similar to the Two-ingredients Appetizer; another ingredient is added in the middle.

拼盤——一般型

轉盤式拼盤製做非常方便，僅需用五或七式
菜餚分裝盤內，美觀而實用，且不需盤飾。

柒星轉盤 A

■ 材料說明：

① 糖酥核桃   ⑤ 椒麻鷄塊
② 薑汁墨魚   ⑥ 水晶牛肉
③ 川味豆魚   ⑦ 糖醋蜇皮
④ 搶黃瓜

五彩轉盤 B

■ 材料說明：

⑧ 糖酥核桃   ⑪ 沙拉火腿
⑨ 薑汁腰片   ⑫ 川味豆魚
⑩ 糖醋蜇塊

APPETIZERS—
POPULAR APPETIZERS

The lazy susan appetizers platter is very easy
to prepare. Place five or seven different
appetizers in the small dishes. This kind of
platter does not need a garnish.

Seven-colors
Lazy Susan A

■ Arranged with:

① Crispy Cashews
② Squid with Ginger Sauce
③ Spicy Flavored Fish
④ Pickled Cucumber
⑤ Spicy Pieces of Chicken
⑥ Sliced Roast Beef
⑦ Jellyfish Salad

Five-flavors
Lazy Susan B

■ Arranged with:

⑧ Crispy Cashews
⑨ Kidney Slices with Ginger Sauce
⑩ Sweet and Sour Jellyfish
⑪ Cooked Chinese Ham
⑫ Spicy Flavored Fish

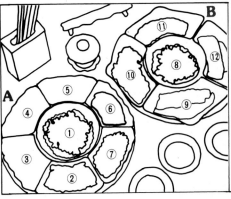

拼盤——一般型

視材料之多寡，選五味或七味堆排在大盤內，其堆排的方式有二(參考第 142 頁和第143頁)。此類拼盤裝盤容易適合一般宴席或家庭採用。

柒味大拼盤 A

■ 材料說明：

① 糖酥核桃　　④ 薰魚　　　⑦ 拌蜇皮
② 餚肉　　　　⑤ 白斬雞　　⑧ 柳丁片
③ 鮑魚　　　　⑥ 五香牛肉　⑨ 櫻桃

五福拼盤 B

■ 材料說明：

① 蘿蔔花 (參考第100頁)　⑥ 薰魚
② 餚肉　　④ 五香牛肉　　⑦ 柳丁片
③ 皮蛋　　⑤ 白斬雞　　　⑧ 櫻桃

APPETIZERS— POPULAR APPETIZERS

Five or seven different ingredients of your preference may be used for this platter. There are two methods to arrange the platter, see pages 142 and 143. These platters are easy to make and often used for family parties.

Seven-flavors Star A

■ Arranged with:

① Crispy Cashews　　　⑦ Jellyfish Salad
② Tasty Chinese Ham Slices
③ Abalone Slices　　　⑧ Orange Slices
④ Smoked Fish　　　　⑨ Cherry
⑤ Pieces of Chicken Meat
⑥ Sliced Five-spice Roast Beef

Five-flavors Plum Blossom B

■ Arranged with:

① Colored White Radish Flower (see p. 100)
② Tasty Chinese Ham Slices
③ Thousand-year Egg Wedges
④ Sliced Five-spice Roast Beef
⑤ Pieces of Chicken Meat　⑦ Orange Slices
⑥ Smoked Fish　　　　　　⑧ Cherry

拼盤──一般型

此二拼盤所用材料大同小異，可隨意用長盤或圓盤，亦可將排式略為改變。

一品拼盤A

■ 材料說明：

① 海蜇皮
② 番茄
③ 鴨肫
④ 明蝦片
⑤ 巴西利
⑥ 洋火腿
⑦ 皮蛋
⑧ 滷鴨
⑨ 五香牛肉
⑩ 鮑魚
⑪ 雞肉

錦繡拼盤B

■ 材料說明：

⑫ 墨魚花（參考第146頁）
⑬ 拌蛋皮
⑭ 明蝦片
⑮ 巴西利
⑯ 櫻桃
⑰ 蛋黃片（參考第128頁）
⑱ 鴨肫
⑲ 小紅蘿蔔
⑳ 雞肉
㉑ 腰子（參考第144頁）
㉒ 紅蘿蔔
㉓ 五香牛肉
㉔ 滷鴨
㉕ 火腿

APPETIZERS— POPULAR APPETIZERS

The ingredients used in these two platters are similar. A round or elongated platter may be used. the arrangement may also vary.

Circles of Delight Platter A

■ Arranged with:

1. Jellyfish Salad
2. Tomato Slices
3. Duck Gizzards
4. Sliced Shrimp
5. Parsley
6. Ham Slices
7. Thousand-year Egg
8. Duck Flavored with Soy Sauce
9. Sliced Five-spice Roast Beef
10. Abalone Slices
11. Chicken Meat

Circles of Grandeur Platter B

■ Arranged with:

12. Squid Flower (see p. 146)
13. Jellyfish Salad
14. Sliced Shrimp
15. Parsley
16. Cherry
17. Slices of Egg Yolk Cake (see p. 128)
18. Duck Gizzards
19. Radish Slices
20. Chicken Meat
21. Kidney (see p. 144)
22. Carrot Strip
23. Sliced Five-spice Roast Beef
24. Duck Flavored with Soy Sauce
25. Cooked Ham

此二拼盤材料非常簡單，僅用粉皮及明蝦薄片再配些盤飾，即可在生日宴席或任何其他宴席上使用。

梅花蝦片 A

■ 材料說明：
① 蘿蔔花 (參考第96頁)　　④ 紅蘿蔔
② 番茄 (參考第67頁)　　　⑤ 明蝦片
③ 黃瓜 (參考第84頁)

壽桃蝦片 B

■ 材料說明：
⑥ 明蝦片　　　　　　　⑧ 紅蘿蔔
⑦ 黃瓜 (第86頁)　　　　⑨ 番茄 (參考第69頁)

APPETIZERS—
POPULAR APPETIZERS

These two platters require only two ingredients—sliced shrimp and vermicelli sheets ("fen pi"). They are accompanied by some garnishes. These platters are usually served for birthday parties.

Plum Blossom Shrimp Platter A

■ Arranged with:
① Colored White Radish Flower (see p. 96)
② Tomato Garnish (see p. 67)
③ Cucumber Garnish (see p. 84)
④ Carrot Strips
⑤ Sliced Shrimp

Long-life Shrimp Platter B

■ Arranged with:
⑥ Sliced Shrimp
⑦ Cucumber Garnish (see p. 86)
⑧ Carrot
⑨ Tomato Garnish (see p. 69)

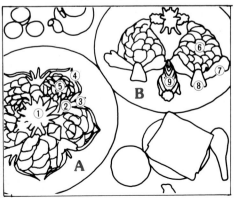

拼盤─四色拼盤

四色拼盤也算是拼盤的一種，將四種菜餚分
裝在四個小碟內，可事先準備好，等客人到
齊時同時上桌，做爲一道前菜。

壽字腰花 A

■ 盤飾：壽字腰花（參考第145 頁）
　　　　蛋黃花（參考第128 頁）

五香牛肉 B

■ 盤飾：小紅蘿蔔花（參考第 122 頁）
　　　　黃瓜（參考第84頁）

滷　　鴨 C

■ 盤飾：染色蘿蔔花（參考第98頁）

塩水胗肝 D

■ 盤飾：小紅蘿蔔花

APPETIZERS—
ASSORTED APPETIZERS

These four platters are served together as
one appetizer at banquets. The platters
can be prepared beforehand. The four
dishes are served when all the guests are
seated.

Long-life
Kidney Platter A

■ Garnish: Long-life Kidney (see p. 122);
Egg Yolk Cake Flower (see p. 128)

Sliced Five-spice
Roast Beef B

■ Garnish: Radish (see p. 122);
Cucumber Garnish (see p. 84)

Duck Flavored with
Soy Sauce C

■ Garnish: Colored White Radish
Flower (see p. 98)

Sliced Gizzards
Platter D

■ Garnish: White Radish Flower

A

C

B

D

40

拼盤—四色拼盤

饈 肉 A

■盤飾：薑切絲，經泡水後整齊矗立在盤邊，並飾以巴西利。

棒 棒 雞 B

■盤飾：蘿蔔蝴蝶（參考第 108 頁）
蘿蔔花（參考第 129 頁）

蜇 皮 捲 C

包心菜燙熟，把蜇皮、紅、白蘿蔔絲、火腿絲等置中間捲好，修齊邊緣，整齊排放在盤上，以紅、綠櫻桃點綴。

五香牛肉 D

■盤飾：黃瓜片圍邊。

APPETIZERS— ASSORTED APPETIZERS

Tasty Chinese Ham Slices A

■ Garnish: Finely slice ginger root and soak it in water. Arrange the thinly-sliced ginger root in a stack, similar to a haystack. Place the ginger root bundle on the sides of the dish; decorate with parsley.

Shredded Chicken Platter B

■ Garnish: White Radish Butterfly (see p. 108), Colored White Radish Flower (see p. 129).

Chinese Cabbage Rolls C

Soak the Chinese cabbage in boiling water until it is cooked. Remove and drain the cabbage leaves. Place shredded jellyfish, carrot, white radish, and ham in the middle of the Chinese cabbage. Roll up the leaf tightly from one end to the other end. Trim the edges and cut it into smaller pieces. Arrange the cabbage rolls on the platter and decorate them with cherry halves.

Sliced Five-spice Roast Beef D

■ Garnish: Arrange overlapping cucumber slices around the platter.

41

C

D

拼盤—四色拼盤

酥炸鳳尾魚 A
■ 盤飾：生菜、番茄皮

滷 鴨 舌 B
■ 盤飾：蘿蔔花（參考第 127 頁）

紅燒冬菇 C
■ 盤飾：蘿蔔花（參考第 99 頁）

銀芽鮑魚絲 D
■ 盤飾：白蘿蔔天鵝（參考第 107 頁）

APPETIZERS— ASSORTED APPETIZERS

Deep-fried Fish Platter A
■ Garnish: Lettuce and tomato skin petals.

Duck Tongues Flavored With Soy Sauce B
■ Garnish: White Radish Flowers (see p. 127).

Chinese Black Mushrooms Dish C
■ Garnish: White Radish Flowers (see p. 99).

Shredded Abalone and Bean Sprouts D
■ Garnish: White Radish Swans (see p. 107), pared cucumber halves.

拼盤—大宴拼盤

鳳鳥来儀

佐用多種材料拼排成華麗的鳳鳥，鳳是中國
古代傳說中的美麗的瑞鳥，象徵吉祥和美滿
婚姻，故多用於婚宴的前菜。

■ 材料說明：

① 腰子（參考第144頁）	⑨ 鴨肉
② 冬菇	⑩ 雞肉
③ 黃瓜	⑪ 筍
④ 蛋黃片（參考第128頁）	⑫ 墨魚花（參考第146頁）
⑤ 櫻桃	⑬ 皮蛋（參考第147頁）
⑥ 鮑魚	⑭ 巴西利
⑦ 黃瓜	⑮ 蛋黃花（參考第128頁）
⑧ 洋火腿	

APPETIZERS— ELEGANT APPETIZER PLATTER

The Arrival Of The Phoenix

The phoenix exists in an ancient Chinese legend. The phoenix is a beautiful bird that brings good luck and happiness to people. It is a good omen that means happiness in marriage. The legend says that when the phoenix comes to you, you will be lucky. When you see the phoenix, you are assured of good luck. Prepare this beautiful phoenix dish for wedding celebrations.

■ Arranged with:

① Kidney (see p. 144)
② Chinese Black Mushroom
③ Cucumber
④ Egg Yolk Cake Slice (see p. 128)
⑤ Cherry   ⑧ Ham
⑥ Abalone   ⑨ Duck Meat
⑦ Cucumber   ⑩ Chicken Meat
⑪ Bamboo Shoot
⑫ Squid Flower (see p. 146)
⑬ Thousand-year Egg (see p. 147)
⑭ Parsley
⑮ Egg Yolk Cake Flower (see p. 128)

梅花拼盤

梅花拼盤是較常見的酒席或宴客前菜，任何
場合均適用。

■ 材料說明：

① 皮蛋（參考第147頁）
② 鮑魚
③ 五香牛肉
④ 滷鴨
⑤ 洋火腿
⑥ 雞肉
⑦ 紅蘿蔔
⑧ 墨魚花（參考第146頁）
⑨ 黃瓜（參考第84頁圖③、④，但黃瓜表面不刻花紋）
⑩ 蘿蔔花（參考第96頁）
⑪ 巴西利

APPETIZERS— ELEGANT APPETIZER PLATTER

Winter Plum Flower

This elegant and colorful cold food
platter is carefully arranged to resemble
the winter plum blossom. It is elegant
enough to be served at any banquet
table.

■ Arranged with:

① Thousand-year Egg (see p. 147)
② Abalone
③ Sliced Five-spice Roast Beef
④ Duck Flavored with Soy Sauce
⑤ Cooked Ham
⑥ Chicken Meat
⑦ Carrot
⑧ Squid Flower (see p. 146)
⑨ Cucumber (see p. 84, Figures ③ and
④, omit the design on the skin)
⑩ White Radish Flower (see p. 96)
⑪ Parsley

松鶴延年

松與鶴均為長壽的象徵，故此道栩栩如生的松鶴拼盤多用於慶壽的宴席上。

■ 材料說明：

① 雞肉
② 鴨肉、火腿
③ 冬菇
④ 鴨肫
⑤ 皮蛋（第147頁）
⑥ 海蜇皮
⑦ 蛋黃花（參考第128頁）
⑧ 櫻桃
⑨ 巴西利
⑩ 紅蘿蔔
⑪ 茄子
⑫ 黃瓜（參考第84頁圖③、④但黃瓜表面不刻花紋）

APPETIZERS— ELEGANT APPETIZER PLATTER
Two Graceful Symbols Of Longevity

The beautiful and graceful crane and pine tree are known for their longevity. This dish is appropriate for birthday celebrations, especially to express blessings to the elderly. Everyone expresses their well wishes by enjoying and sharing this dish.

■ Arranged with:

① Chicken Meat
② Duck Meat and cooked Ham
③ Chinese Black Mushroom
④ Duck Gizzards
⑤ Thousand-year Egg (see p. 147)
⑥ Shredded Jellyfish
⑦ Egg Yolk Cake Flower (see p. 128)
⑧ Cherry
⑨ Parsley
⑩ Carrot
⑪ Eggplant
⑫ Cucumber (see p. 84, Figures③ and ④, omit the design on the skin).

花籃拼盤

此種色彩明艷生動的花籃拼盤，是一道誘人的前菜，適用於各種宴席。

■ 材料說明：

① 黃 瓜（參考第86頁） ⑧ 鴨胸肉
② 墨 魚（參考第146頁） ⑨ 熟紅蘿蔔
③ 鮑 魚（參考第128頁） ⑩ 五香牛肉
④ 洋火腿（參考第128頁） ⑪ 巴西利
⑤ 蘿蔔花（參考第128頁） ⑫ 拌蜇皮
⑥ 蛋黃花（參考第128頁）
⑦ 腰 子（參考第146頁）

APPETIZERS— ELEGANT APPETIZER PLATTER

A Basket Of Spring Flowers

Present this beautiful basket of colorful edible flowers at any festive dinner or banquet. Express your congratulations and best wishes with a different kind of basket of flowers.

■ Arranged with:

① Cucumber (see p. 86)
② Squid Flower (see p. 146)
③ Abalone Flower (see p. 128)
④ Cooked Ham Flower (see p. 128)
⑤ Carrot Flower (see p. 128)
⑥ Egg Yolk Cake Flower (see p. 128)
⑦ Kidney Flower (see p. 146)
⑧ Duck Meat
⑨ Cooked Carrot
⑩ Sliced Five-spice Roast Beef
⑪ Parsley
⑫ Jellyfish Salad

餐盤裝飾—特殊

雞　群 A

一對公雞和母雞身體強壯，
小雞純潔可愛，嬉戲在雙親身邊，
滿幸福的家庭。

■ 材料說明：

①金錢蝦

GARNISHES — SPECIAL GARNISHES

Spring Is Everywhere A

A rooster and a hen watch while their chicks play under their loving attention.

■ Arranged with:

① Golden Shrimp Balls
② White Radish
③ Carrot and matchsticks (see p. 104)
④ Carrot
⑤ Cherry
⑥ Orange Garnish (see p. 91, Vegetable Marrow Garnish 1, Figures ② and ③).
⑦ Tomato
⑧ Lettuce

APPETIZERS— ELEGANT APPETIZER PLATTER

The Proud Peacock B

The peacock displays its pride by spreading its feathers in an array of splendid colors. This arrangement is used to express good wishes on the occasion of a grand opening of a business. It is an expression of good wishes for a successful future.

■ Arranged with:

⑨ Carrot
⑩ Carrot and matchstick (see p. 104)
⑪ White Radish, Carrot and Cucumber (see p. 135)
⑫ Abalone
⑬ Chinese Sausage and Pork Liver
⑭ Cucumber
⑮ Cherry
⑯ Asparagus
⑰ Shrimp
⑱ Steamed Pork with Salty Egg Yolk
⑲ Pork heart
⑳ Parsley

拼盤—大宴拼盤

錦繡雀屏B

孔雀只有在它最快樂的時候才會把尾羽豎起並且張開，顯示出它最美麗的青春，象徵開張大吉，前程似錦。

■ 材料說明：
⑨紅蘿蔔
⑩紅蘿蔔、火柴棒（參考第104頁）。
⑪白、紅蘿蔔、黃瓜（參考第135頁）。
⑫鮑魚
⑬香腸、豬肝
⑭黃瓜
⑮櫻桃
⑯蘆筍
⑰明蝦
⑱蛋黃肉
⑲猪心
⑳巴西利

滿，兩隻
，象徵美

。

·（③）

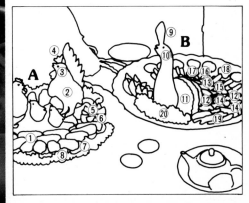

龍舟競渡

中國民間習俗有於農曆端午節舉行龍舟競賽
的遊藝節目。此拼盤宜用於端午節前後舉辦
之筵席。

■ 材料說明：

龍舟做法參考第106頁。

① 紅蘿蔔
② 紅蘿蔔、火柴棒（參考第104頁）
③ 白蘿蔔　　　⑦ 烏魚子
④ 櫻桃　　　　⑧ 青蒜
⑤ 黑棗　　　　⑨ 包心菜
⑥ 竹製水果叉　⑩ 柳丁片

APPETIZERS—
ELEGANT APPETIZER
PLATTER

The Dragon Yacht Race

It is a Chinese tradition to hold a yacht
racing event every year during the fifth
moon. This platter arrangement is
usually prepared for this occasion. The
motif of the arrangement reminds
people of the race and all its exciting
events.

■ Arranged with:

See p. 106 for the directions to make the
Dragon Yacht.

① Carrot
② Carrot and matchstick (see p. 104)
③ White Radish
④ Cherry
⑤ Prunes　　　　⑧ Scallion
⑥ Bamboo Fork　⑨ Chinese Cabbage
⑦ Dried Fish Eggs　⑩ Orange Slice

藍橋相會

一對天鵝在橋上相會，使人聯想起唐朝裴航
在藍橋遇見美麗的仙女雲英，逐成眷屬升天
成仙的故事，象徵着美滿姻緣。

■ 材料說明：

天鵝做法參考第107頁。

① 紅辣椒
② 火柴棒
③ 白蘿蔔
④ 紅蘿蔔
⑤ 番茄（參考第75頁）
⑥ 黃瓜、紅蘿蔔（參考第133頁）
⑦ 紙包雞

APPETIZERS— ELEGANT APPETIZER PLATTER

Meeting At Blue Bridge

There is a Chinese legend about a
handsome young man ·who met a
beautiful and enchanting young girl on
Blue Bridge. The two young lovers
married and flew to heaven. Flying to
heaven means that they would never
die. This dish symbolizes the two lovers
meeting on the bridge and reaching out
for each other. The dish represents
longevity and happiness in marriage.

■ Arranged with:

See p. 107 for the directions to make the
swans.

① Red pepper
② Matchstick
③ White Radish
④ Carrot
⑤ Tomato Garnish (see p. 75)
⑥ Cucumber and Carrot (see p. 133)
⑦ Paper-wrapped Fried Chicken

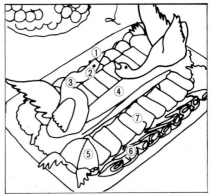

拼盤—大宴拼盤

永矢同心 A

史記記載西漢時四川臨邛富豪卓王孫的女兒
文君"新寡，好音"因爲愛慕文學家司馬相如
，亡奔相如，相如乃與馳歸……才子佳人
珠聯璧合傳爲佳話。

■ 材料說明：
① 白蘿蔔　⑥ 番茄
② 葱　　　⑦ 紅辣椒
③ 櫻桃　　⑧ 黃瓜
④ 黑棗　　⑨ 巴西利
⑤ 紅蘿蔔　⑩ 明蝦酥餅

一帆風順 B

寓意祝福事業順利或旅途平安。

帆船做法參考第105頁。

龍柱呈祥 C

龍柱是中國宮殿建築藝術之一，象徵吉祥

■ 材料說明：
① 紅蘿蔔
② 柳丁（參考第91頁胡瓜盤飾圖②、③）
③ 染色白蘿蔔
④ 炸蝦片
⑤ 大黃瓜
⑥ 生菜
⑦ 巴西利

APPETIZERS— ELEGANT APPETIZER PLATTER

Lend A Note Of Love and Unity A

This garnish represents a very popular love story in China about Chu Wen-Chun, a famous widow, who eloped with Sze Ma Hsian Zo of the Han Dynasty.

■ Arranged with:

① White Radish
② Scallion
③ Cherry
④ Prunes
⑤ Carrot
⑥ Tomato
⑦ Red pepper
⑧ Cucumber
⑨ Parsley
⑩ Crispy Shrimp Cakes

Bon Voyage B

This dish is used to express good wishes for a peaceful and safe journey. See p. 105 for the directions to make the san pan.

The Dragon Pillar C

The dragon pillar is often used in Chinese temple architectural art. The dragon pillars are symbols of good luck and happiness.

■ Arranged with:

① Carrot
② Orange Garnish (see p. 91 Vegetable Marrow Garnish , Figures ② and ③)
③ Colored White Radish
④ Fried Shrimp Slice
⑤ Cucumber
⑥ Lettuce
⑦ Parsley

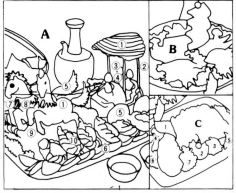

彩蝶飛

一雙彩蝶雙棲雙飛，恰如一對恩愛夫妻相依相隨。
此道拼盤的變化較多，是應用本書中所介紹過的一些盤飾和拼盤來做的。
這類拼盤本無固定之模式，只要經常練習和觀摩，便能融會貫通，
隨手做來即成一道栩栩如生的拼盤。

APPETIZERS—
ELEGANT APPETIZER
PLATTER

Two Butterflies

Their closeness symbolizes the close union of a
couple that is in love. The garnishes and appetizers
are presented in another section of this book
and may be adapted and combined to prepare this intricate butterfly platter.
This platter does not follow a specific
pattern. You will be
able to create your
own patterns through
observation and
practice.

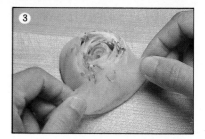

① 將蘋果切半，再切薄片，略泡鹽水使變軟。
② 取一片捲成花心。
③ 皮面朝下倒放在檯上，將蘋果片順序包裹在花心上。
④ 全部包裹好，用刀面剷起。
⑤ 將花面倒轉朝上即成花朵。
⑥ 其他蔬果可切片者，均可使用。例如：番茄、柳丁、蘿蔔等。

① Cut an apple in half lengthwise. Turn the apple half cut side down; cut it lengthwise into paper-thin slices. Soak the apple slices in lightly salted water until they become pliable.
② Take one apple slice and crosswise roll it up like a jelly roll. This will be the center of the flower.
③ Turn the rolled apple slice skin side down. (You will be working with the apple slices skin side down.) Arrange the remaining slices around the apple center, skin side down.
④ Use the flat side of a cleaver to lift the apple garnish.
⑤ Carefully turn the garnish over to its upright position.
⑥ You may use other fruits or vegetables such as tomatoes, oranges, or a white radish that can be sliced in the prescribed manner.

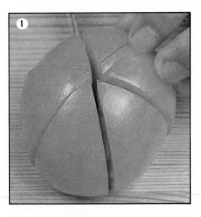

① 番茄去頭，底朝上，切成六等份。

② 每份中間切ㄑ形深約0.3～0.4公分。

③ 將皮片開至⅔處。

④ 輕輕撥開成花瓣狀。每份可單獨使用，亦可半個或整個使用。

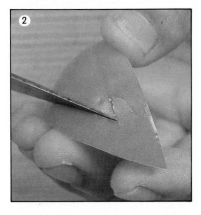

① Cut off a thin slice from the stem end of the tomato. Turn the tomato cut side down; then cut it into six wedges.

② In the middle, on the skin side, of each tomato wedge, make two cuts 1/8 to 1/6 inch deep to form a v-shape. The point of the "v" should face the narrow end of the tomato wedge.

③ Use a paring knife to separate the skin, and the meat which is attached to the skin, from the rest of the tomato. Start cutting at the pointed end and continue cutting to two-thirds of the length of the tomato wedge.

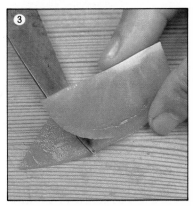

④ Gently bend back the skin from the rest of the wedge to form a petal. Repeat the process for the remaining tomato wedges. Gather together the wedges to form the original tomato shape. A wedge may be set flat on the side of a plate to serve as a simple garnish or a pair of wedges, pointed toward each other may be used.

① 番茄去頭，底朝上，在面上劃十字刀痕長至 $\frac{2}{3}$ 處。
② 將皮片開至 $\frac{1}{2}$ 處，輕輕撥開成花瓣狀。
③ 中央用筷子穿洞。
④ 蔥枝將葉子略修剪，根部斜切尖，插入番茄內。
⑤ 亦可將皮片開成各種不同的形狀。
⑥ 或將番茄囊挖空，其內可放些櫻桃點綴或盛放沾料。

① Cut off a thin slice of the tomato at the stem end so that the tomato will sit flat on the plate. Outline a cross by piercing the skin only. The cuts should extend to two-thirds of the length of the tomato.

② Use a paring knife to carefully lift the tip of the tomato skin at the center of the cross; then carefully separate the skin, and the meat that is attached, from the rest of the tomato to about half the length of the tomato. Repeat this procedure with the other three petals (flaps).

③ Gently pierce the top center of the tomato to make a hole.

④ Make a few vertical cuts along the length of the green end of a scallion so that it will "bloom". Place the scallion in water to allow it to blossom further. Remove and drain. Diagonally trim the white tip of the scallion to make a pointed end; then stick it into the tomato, as illustrated. Place several leaves of lettuce on the serving plate and set the tomato garnish in the center of the leaves. OR

⑤ The tomato skin may be cut in several ways to achieve the designs that are illustrated. OR

⑥ Hollow out the tomato and fill it with a dipping sauce.

①取番茄半個,在離中心點各0.2公分處,以斜刀交切。

②以同樣方法,每隔0.5公分連續切數層,最後一刀斜切之交會點在中心,並切斷。

③將底端兩片取出,順皮片開至⅔處,再放回原位。

④由第一片向前推出0.5公分,以此類推向前,使呈桃形狀。

⑤底端兩片,皮不片開亦可。

⑥或將底端兩片,再依同法切出反方向的桃形。

① Cut a tomato in half lengthwise. Turn the tomato cut side down. Make a diagonal cut toward the center and about 1/8 inch from the middle of the tomato half. On the other side, 1/4 inch from the first cut, make another diagonal cut down toward the center of the tomato. Both cuts should meet and form a wedge.

② Make several diagonal cuts in the same manner at 1/4-inch intervals. The final cuts will produce two wedges.

③ Remove the two wedges. Starting at the pointed end, cut the skin, and attached meat, down to two-thirds of the length of the tomato wedge. Gently bend back the skin from the rest of the wedge to form a petal. Repeat this procedure with the other wedge. Return the wedges to their original place.

④ Gently move each tomato slice, as illustrated, to form a "tiers" (layers). OR

⑤ Leave the two bottom wedges intact. OR

⑥ The two wedges may be cut as in Steps ① - ② and placed on both sides of the other "tiered" slices but pointing toward the opposite direction.

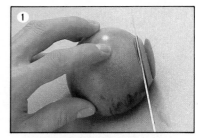
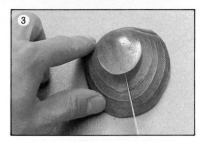

① 番茄去頭，底朝上，每隔0.5公分深切一刀，不切斷。

② 連續切四刀，第五刀切斷。

③ 將籽挖除，由第二片中心，直切到底。

④ 用刀面輕輕拍扁，使呈螃蟹狀。

⑤ 另切一公分厚片，再切開成兩半，每半均片薄皮至⅔處，相對擺成蝴蝶狀，即可使用。

⑥ 或將蟹狀盤飾覆蓋其上使用亦可。

① Cut off a thin slice from the stem end of a tomato. Turn the tomato cut side down; then slice at 1/4-inch intervals but do not cut through to the bottom.

② Continue to slice only four slices; cut through to the bottom after the fourth slice.

③ Remove the seeds. Turn the joined tomato slices skin side up. Starting at the center of the second slice from the stem end, cut the slices in half.

④ Use the flat side of the knife to gently press the tomato slices to form a crab. OR

⑤ Cut one more slice of tomato then cut it in half. Peel the skin, and the meat that is attached, from the curved end almost to the other end. Arrange the tomato halves to resemble a butterfly. This garnsih may be used alone. OR

⑥ Put the crab-shaped tomato garnish on top of the butterfly garnish, as shown.

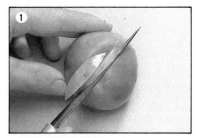

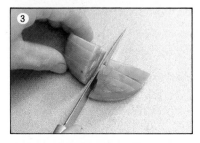

①番茄去頭，底朝上，在離中心點各0.2公分處以斜刀交切。

②以同樣方法連續切四層取出。

③橫切兩半。

④另餘下部份兩側也分別切半，但不切斷。

⑤每半均片開薄皮，並在皮上刻鋸齒花紋。

⑥將切出之部份放回原位，並依層次向外推出。

① Cut off a thin slice from the stem end of a tomato. Turn the tomato cut side down. Make a diagonal cut down toward the center and about 1/8 inch from the middle of the tomato' half. On the other side, 1/4 inch from the first cut, make another diagonal cut down toward the center of the tomato. Both cuts should meet and produce a wedge.

② Diagonally cut two more slices on both sides at 1/4-inch intervals.

③ Turn the sliced tomato wedge on its side and cut it in half crosswise.

④ Take the remaining tomato and cut both sides in half where the sliced wedge was removed—do not cut through to the other side (see illustration).

⑤ Use a paring knife to carefully separate the skin, and the attached meat, from the rest of the tomato to form a petal. Cut v-shaped grooves around each tomato petal.

⑥ Arrange the sliced wedge, previously cut in Steps ① - ③ in the center of the tomato. Gently move the slices away from the center to give a "tier" (or layer) or "diamond" effect as shown.

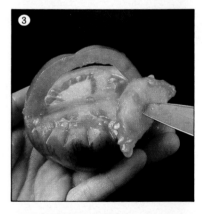

①番茄去頭，底朝上，在離中心點各0.5公分處切兩直刀至半腰，再橫切兩刀，去除兩塊。

②沿籃邊刻鋸齒花紋。

③挖去籃把中間多餘的囊肉。

④將籃內的囊肉挖除，再插些小花點綴。

① Cut off a thin slice from the stem end of the tomato. Turn the tomato stem end down. Cut 1/4 inch from the center of the tomato down to the middle of the tomato. On the opposite side, 1/2 inch away from the previous cut, make another cut. This will be the handle.

② Cut deep v-shaped grooves around the middle of the tomato, from the bottom of the handle to the other side of the handle. Remove this portion. Repeat this step for the other side of the handle.

③ Remove the seeds and meat of the tomato from the section that forms the handle.

④ Hollow out the center of the tomato. Vegetable flowers may be placed in the center of the tomato basket as illustrated.

①由番茄底端片切1.5公分寬之薄皮。

②連續不斷將整個番茄皮片成一長條。

③由底端開始捲起。

④環繞成花朵狀。

① Use a paring knife to slice a paper-thin piece of skin 5/8 inch wide at the non stem end of the tomato; do not cut it off. It will be one end of the spiral.

② Starting at the 5/8 inch piece of skin, remove the rest of the skin in one spiral by cutting in a circular fashion around the tomato until you have one long strip.

③ Take the end of the strip then carefully wind it around itself. The end will be the center of the flower.

④ Continue to wind the rest of the skin around itself; then shape it into a flower.

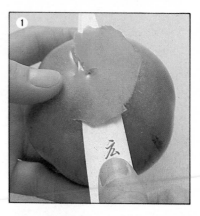

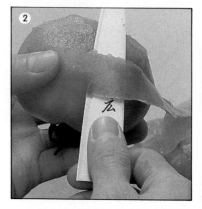

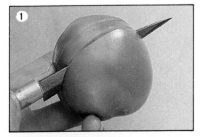

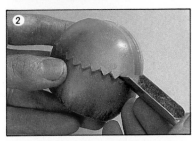

① 番茄去頭，底朝上，在離中心點各0.5公分處切兩直刀至半腰。

② 由兩側深刻鋸齒紋，取下上端兩塊留用。

③ 挖除籽，順鋸齒紋在番茄面劃直刀。

④ 將皮片開。

⑤ 用手輕輕撥開。

⑥ 留用的兩塊，片下薄皮，擺飾在花籃兩旁。

① Cut off a thin slice from the stem end of the tomato. Turn the tomato stem end down. Cut 1/4 inch from the center of the tomato down to the middle of the tomato. On the opposite side, 1/2 inch away from the previous cut, make another cut. This will be the handle.

② Cut deep v-shaped grooves around the middle of the tomato, from handle to handle. Remove and retain this portion. Repeat this step for the other side of the handle.

③ Remove the seeds. Starting at the point of each v-groove, vertically score the skin of the tomato.

④ Separate the skin, and attached meat, from the rest of the tomato.

⑤ Use your fingers to separate the petals from the meat of the tomato.

⑥ Use a knife to remove the meat from the skin of the two wedges taken to form the handle. Place the two pieces of tomato skin under the tomato garnish to serve as an added decoration.

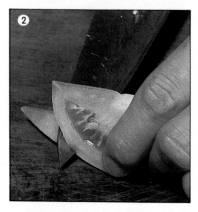

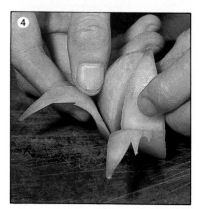

①番茄去頭，切成四等份。
②取一份再切兩半，每半由尾端片薄皮至￼處。
③薄皮一邊修成鋸齒狀。
④輕輕將皮撥開，兩半組合置於盤邊。

① Cut off a slice from the stem end of the tomato. Turn the tomato stem end down; then cut it into four quarters.
② Cut one wedge in half lengthwise. Use a paring knife to separate the skin and attached meat. Start at the pointed end of the half wedge.
③ Diagonally cut a few long v-shaped grooves on one side of the petal.
④ Use your fingers to separate the petal from the meat of the tomato. Put two wedges together and place them to a side in the serving dish.

①取茄子一段，切成五瓣（底部不切斷）。
②兩瓣間切除∨形小塊，花瓣頂端亦修成∨形。
③順着皮片出一層花瓣。
④頂部略修整，泡水後使用。
⑤⑥或將花瓣頂端修尖，順皮片出二層花瓣，再將內層花瓣摺起即成。

① Use a three-inch section of eggplant. Cut the top of the eggplant into five sections, as illustrated. Do not cut down through to the other end of the eggplant.
② Carve a small v-shaped groove in the middle of each of the five sections. The cut should extend from the edge to the center of the eggplant section. Carve out the wedge from each section to form a large v-shaped petal.
③ Use a paring knife to separate the skin from the meat of the eggplant.
④ Sculpt the inside of the eggplant, as illustrated. Soak the garnish in water until ready for use. OR
⑤⑥ Cut six inverted "v's" around one end of the eggplant. At each point, cut back the skin of each v-shaped section. Cut a second (white) layer of v-shaped petals as before. Fold the white petal in toward the center of the eggplant.

①取茄子一段，切成四瓣（底部不切斷），每瓣均修尖。

②每瓣上斜切兩刀成人形。

③順着皮片出花瓣。

④共片出二層花瓣。

⑤將第一層花瓣往內摺。

⑥第二層花瓣亦往內摺起。將中央略切短並插入紅辣椒點綴即成。

①Use a three-inch section of eggplant for this garnish. Make two intersecting cuts across one end of the eggplant to serve as guidelines. Cut a long narrow inverted "v" on the length of each (quarter) section. Remove the narrow wedge that is formed.

②Inside each inverted v-shaped section, diagonally make two slits like an inverted "v".

③Use a paring knife to carefully separate the skin from the meat of the eggplant along the inverted "v" sections.

④Carve one more row of petals behind each dark petal.

⑤Bend the dark petal toward the center to hold it in place.

⑥Bend the white petal in toward the center to hold it in place. Trim the center to a shorter length; and trim the tip to a point. Red pimento may be placed in the center of the garnish to add color.

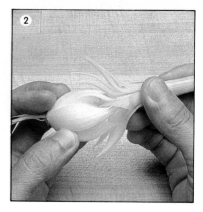

① 葱取根部一段，在葱頭周圍斜刀交切成鋸齒狀（刻四或五瓣，可視葱頭的大小決定）。

② 將葱頭分開成兩半。

③ 將葱瓣用手輕輕撥開。

④ 泡水或泡在染料內，即展開成花朵。

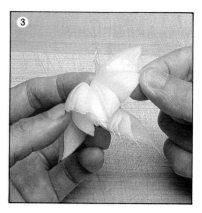

① Use the white part of the scallion for this garnish. Lengthwise make deep petal-shaped cuts into the center of the bulb of the scallion. The tips of the petals should point toward the non stem end. Cut 4 or 5 petals (the number of petals may vary depending on the size of the scallion).

② To separate, pull out the carved end (stem end) from the rest of the scallion, as illustrated.

③ Use your fingers to carefully separate the petals of the flower.

④ Soak the flower garnish in water until petals open.

① 沿洋葱底用尖形刀雕一圈花瓣。

② 在表皮輕劃一刀。

③ 剝去一層。

④ 同法再雕出第二層花瓣，如此反覆數層即成花朵，泡水後使用。

① Remove the skin from the onion. Use a sharp instrument to carve v-shaped petals around the non stem end of the onion.

② Lengthwise score the surface of the upper part of the onion.

③ Remove the top layer of the large section of onion.

④ Carve a second row of petals as in Step ①. Score the surface of the upper part of the onion; remove this layer. Continue carving petals until the onion is completely carved. Place the onion in water and let it soak until ready for use.

①大黃瓜縱剖成兩半，再削去有籽的部份。斜刀切除尾端後，片切 0.1 公分
之薄片，一端留 1 公分不切斷，切 5 或 7 片爲一組（成奇數片）。

②間隔內摺後，泡水使用。

③在表皮上刻直條花紋。

④切法與①相同，輕拍成扇型。

① Lengthwise cut a cucumber in half. Lengthwise cut off a slice thick
enough to remove the seeds. Diagonally cut off the tip of the narrow
end of the cucumber. Diagonally cut a paper-thin slice; do not cut
through. Continue to cut 5 or 7 slices in the same manner so that all
slices are joined at the bottom. After the fifth or seventh slice, cut
completely through to separate the sliced section from the rest of
the cucumber.

② Starting with the second slice, bend every other slice toward the
joined end of the cucumber to hold it securely in place. Place the
cucumber in water and let it soak until ready for use. OR

③ To prepare a variation of the above pattern: Cut a cucumber
Lengthwise in half. Lengthwise cut off a slice thick enough to remove
the seeds. On the skin side, cut out v-shaped grooves across the
cucumber half.

④ Cut the slices as directed in Step ①. Use the flat side of the blade of a
cleaver or knife to gently press the cucumber slices so that they "fan"
out. Place the garnish in water and let it soak for several minutes.

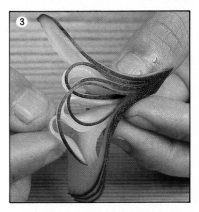

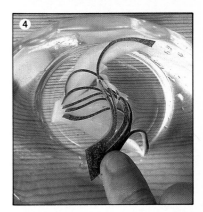

① 大黃瓜縱剖成兩半、削去籽，斜刀切除尾端後，切薄片 7 或 9 片為一組，一端不切斷。

② 由未切的一端，將皮片開至⅘處。

③ 兩頭不摺，餘均內摺。

④ 泡水後使用。

① Cut a cucumber in half lengthwise; cut off a slice thick enough to remove the seeds. Diagonally cut off the tip of the narrow end of the cucumber. Diagonally cut 7 or 9 paper-thin slices, do not cut through. Cut through after the seventh or ninth slice to separate the sliced section from the rest of the cucumber.

② Place the sliced cucumber section on a flat surface, skin side down. Start to cut the skin away from the meat at the joined end; carefully slice to four-fifths of the length of the cucumber.

③ Bend the second slice and every other slice in toward the joined end; leave the two slices at both ends straight.

④ Place the garnish in water and let it soak for 10 minutes before using.

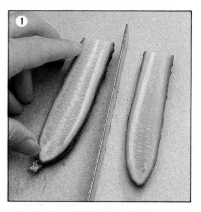

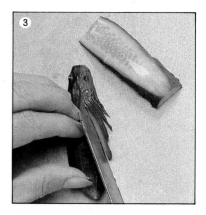

①黃瓜切除一端，再縱剖爲兩半。
②每半由切口處向尾端斜切。
③順尾端片切薄片。
④輕輕拍扁即成。

① Remove the stem end of a cucumber then cut it lengthwise in half.
② Turn the cucumber half cut side down on a flat surface. Starting at the straight end, place the cutting blade at an angle with the sharp edge under the skin. Diagonally cut to the other end. The skin piece will be thin at the starting point and thick at the end of the cut.
③ Turn the cucumber skin side up. Place the cutting blade at a slant near the thin end. Carefully cut paper-thin slices, do not cut through.
④ Use the flat side of a cleaver to gently press the cucumber slices so that they will "fan" out.

①大黃瓜取尾段（長約15公分），切半，修成龍蝦尾狀。

②沿尾端邊緣片開 0.1公分薄皮。

③前端兩側各切出四片，最外一片不動，餘均切短 1 公分。靠內兩側再各切除一小塊使蝦頭略尖。

④蝦頭兩側各切出二條鬚，將頭修尖，並在邊緣上刻鋸齒花紋。

⑤蝦頭和鬚均片出 0.1公分薄皮。

⑥蝦身刻些橫條紋，蝦頭刻∨形並用刀將皮片開呈刺紋。火柴棒套上紅辣椒片做眼睛，再把兩側蝦腳內三片摺起，泡水後使用。

① Trim a cucumber to a section seven or eight inches long. Cut the section in half lengthwise; turn the section skin side up. Cut out a v-shaped grooves at the end. Trim the sides of the cucumber to curve in at the end. Cut out smaller v-shaped grooves on both sides of the larger v-shaped groove.

② On the underside, separate the cucumber meat and the skin at the "tail end" of the cucumber (lobster). Carve completely around and under the rounded edge.

③ Turn the cucumber so that the "head" faces you. Lengthwise cut four thin slices on both sides. Trim 1/3 inch off the ends of the three inside slices. Vertically cut two, 1/4 inch thick, v-shaped wedges from the tip of the cucumber. Remove the wedges.

④ Cut two slices on both sides of the head to form the tentacles. Carve the head to a point. Carve small v-shaped grooves along the pointed end.

⑤ Cut the skin of the head and tentacles away from the meat and bend the skin upward.

⑥ Carve small v-shaped grooves into the skin of the cucumber from the head back to the middle of the section. Bend the tips of the grooves upward. Carve straight lines on the remaining half of the section. Cut two small circles out of red pepper to be used for the eyes. Secure the eyes to the body with the tips of two wooden matchsticks. Fold the three inside slices on each side of the cucumber in toward the body.

■ A zucchini may also be used for this garnish.

①大黃瓜切半再切成梯形，兩側各切出四片。

②前端切除三角形小塊。

③修成蟹螯。

④將頭部修圓並刻鋸齒花紋。

⑤在蟹身刻 S 形花紋。

⑥用火柴頭做眼睛，兩側蟹腳內三片摺起，泡水後使用。

① Cut a cucumber lengthwise in half. Cut one of the halves, at opposite angles, into thirds (△). Turn the center section so that the longest edge is closest to you then cut four thin slices on both sides to 1/4 inch from the opposite (narrow) edge.

② Cut out a triangle from the center of the longest side, the point of the triangle should point toward the long edge.

③ At an angle, cut out a long, narrow v-shaped wedge on the inside of the cucumber (where the triangle was removed) to form the front claws.

④ Trim the edge between the two front claws to a curve and cut out v-shaped grooves along the curve.

⑤ Carve an elongated "s" on the surface of the body; remove the skin from the carved "s".

⑥ Use the tips of two wooden matchsticks to make the eyes. Bend in the three inside slices on both sides of the cucumber crab.

■ A zucchini may also be used for this garnish.

黄瓜盤飾・Cucumber Garnish

6

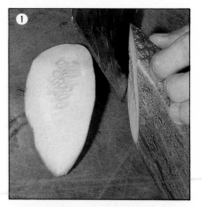

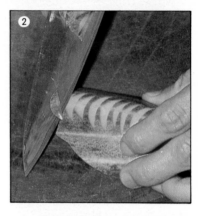

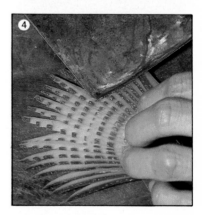

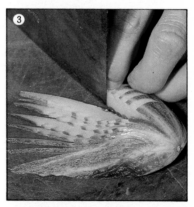

①斜切取大黃瓜頭部一段。
②在皮上斜刀刻除6－8片半月形小片。
③片薄片，頂端不切斷。
④以刀面推壓或輕拍成扇型即成。

①Diagonally cut off a three-inch section from either end of a cucumber. The end being cut off will be used for this garnish.
②Place the cucumber end, cut side down, on a flat surface. Cut small wedges across the center of the section; remove the excess cucumber.
③Starting close to the thick end, lengthwise cut paper-thin strips.
④Use the flat side of a cleaver to gently press the cucumber strips to "fan" them out.

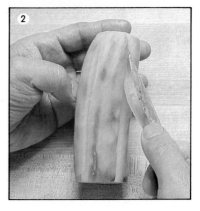

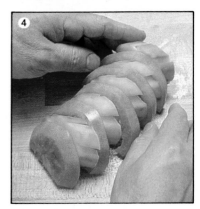

①小黃瓜去皮，稍留些綠色在瓜面上。
②在瓜面刻出數條直溝。
③斜切薄片，即可用來做盤飾。
④或將黃瓜片與番茄片間隔排列，用來做菜餚的圍邊。

① Pare the cucumber. Leave some of the skin, if desired.
② Cut long v-shaped strips around the length of the cucumber.
③ Diagonally cut 1/4 inch slices across the cucumber.
④ Tomato slices may be placed between the cucumber slices for an added touch of color.

① 沿胡瓜底雕一圈細長花瓣。
② 順細長花瓣下方，斜刀深刻一圈鋸齒形。
③ 剝離開。
④ 在中央隨意點綴一朵紅花即成。

① Use a sharp instrument to carve deep, long, narrow, v-shaped petals around the non stem end of the vegetable marrow. The top of the petals should point toward the stem end of the squash.
② Cut larger v-shaped petals behind the first row of petals. The cuts should reach the center of the squash.
③ Separate the two sections of squash.
④ Another smaller garnish may be placed in the center of the squash to add a finishing touch and color to this garnish.

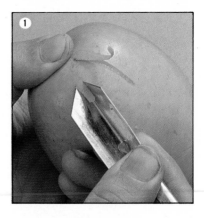

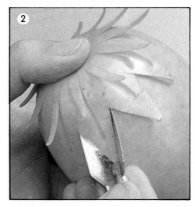

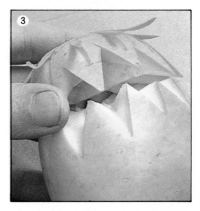

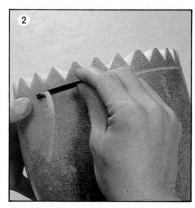

① 取冬瓜頭一段，沿瓜緣刻鋸齒花紋。

② 用雕花刀由右向左推進，雕出一條細紋。

③ 上緣雕出萬字花紋，近底部也雕一圈萬字紋，中間雕壽字，最後挖去囊肉和籽即成。

④ 亦可雕成福祿壽圖案。

① Use half of a winter squash for this garnish. This garnish is used as a serving tureen. The choice of size of the squash will depend on the quantity of food being served. Carve v-shaped grooves around the rim of the squash, as shown.

② Use a sharp cutting instrument to lightly outline a thin continuous line; just below the v-shaped grooves, around the squash.

③ Outline and carve the borders. Outline and carve the "long life" design. Hollow out the squash. OR

④ Carve the Chinese characters signifying fortune, prosperity, and longevity on the squash, as shown.

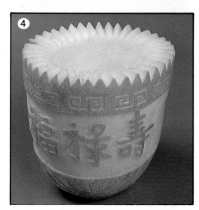

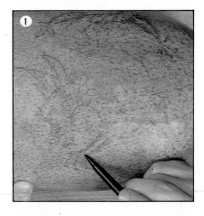

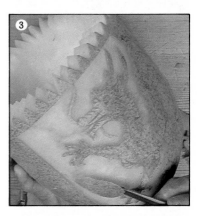

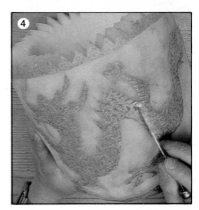

① 取冬瓜頭一段（長約20公分），先用筆在冬瓜皮上描繪龍形。

② 挖除瓜籽及部份瓜肉，使空間較大，以便放置作料。沿瓜緣刻鋸齒紋。

③④將龍形四周之瓜皮刻除，使龍形現出。

① This garnish is used as a serving tureen. Use half of a winter squash for this garnish. Sketch the outline of a dragon on the skin of the squash.

② Remove the seeds and hollow out most of the center so that it will hold more soup. Carve v-shaped grooves around the edge of the squash.

③④ Pare the mellon where necessary to finish the dragon design. Carve out the scales of the dragon. If winter squash is unavailable, a hollowed out watermelon may be used.

① 芋頭去皮修成圓筒狀，先切去十塊如圖 ，再將高起的一邊修圓如圖 。
② 在較高的圓弧上刻波浪紋 ，再由兩邊切 0.2 公分寬之兩刀，呈 。
③ 切 0.1 公分厚之薄片，第一刀切至離底部 0.5 公分處，不切斷，第二刀
　 切斷，兩片為一組。
④ 每組在相連的底部斜切一刀如圖 。
⑤⑥ 用雙手，一手捏住底部，另一手將蝶頭往上提起（有波浪紋的一端為
　 蝶頭），插入另端，疊成蝴蝶狀。泡水後使用。

① Remove the skin from a medium-size taro root; trim the taro root to
　 smooth the surface. Cut out and remove a quarter section down
　 the length of the taro root. Trim the sharp edge of the root to round
　 out the shape ( ).
② Carve out v-shaped grooves on the top edge of the taro section
　 ( ). Make one diagonal cut on the side where the grooves were
　 made. Make a straight cut into the opposite side of the taro, as illus-
　 trated ( ).
③ Cut a slice about 1/8 inch thick, cutting just short of the opposite
　 edge. Make a second cut 1/8 inch from the first cut, cutting all the
　 way through.
④ On the connected edge of the double slice, make a diagonal cut,
　 cutting past the center of the section ( ).
⑤⑥ While holding the half slice at the connected edge, lift the grooved
　 side and rest it on the opposite side. When open it will resemble a
　 butterfly.

白蘿蔔盤飾・White Radish Garnish (Daikon)

1

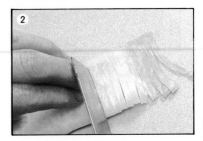

①取白蘿蔔中段長約10公分，去皮修成圓筒狀，旋轉片出長條薄片（約30公分）。抹些鹽使軟化。

②對摺後，在摺起的一邊每隔 0.3 公分切開，頂端留 1 公分不切斷。

③由一端捲起成花朵狀，底部插上牙籤固定之。

④泡水或泡入染料內，即展開成花朵。

⑤或將蘿蔔片對摺後，在摺起的一邊每隔 0.3 公分切開，前三刀切直刀做花心的部份，其餘均切斜刀，捲成花朵，在花心染上顏色。

⑥或將蘿蔔片對摺後，在摺起的一邊，先隔 0.5 公分切兩直刀做花心的部份，其餘每隔 1 公分斜切，捲起成花朵。

①Cut off the ends of a white radish; trim the radish to four inches long. Pare the radish. Hold the cutting knife parallel to the radish; then peel off a long, thin, continuous slice about 12 inches long. Rub a little salt on the radish slice; let it stand for about 10 minutes or until it becomes pliable.

②Fold the radish slice in half lengthwise. Cut 1/8 inch wide strips across the fold, slice to within 1/3 inch from the long open edges.

③Take one end of the folded radish strip and roll it like a jelly roll. Secure the ends with a toothpick.

④Soak the radish in water; food coloring may be added to the water. OR

⑤Fold the sliced radish in half lengthwise. Make three 1/8 inch cuts across the fold to within 1/3 inch from the long open edges. The remaining cuts are made diagonally 1/8 inch wide. Start to roll up the radish slice at the first three cuts. (This will be the center of the flower.) And roll it like a jelly roll. OR

⑥Fold the sliced radish in half lengthwise. Make two 1/6 inch wide cuts across the fold to within 1/3 inch from the long open edges. Diagonally cut the remaining radish strip into 1/3 inch wide strips. Start to roll up the radish slice at the first two cuts; this will be the center of the flower.

① 取白蘿蔔根部（或頭部）一段，沿圓周切除六片。
② 在同位置內側再刻一刀，刻出第一層花瓣。
③ 沿圓周挖除一圈多餘部份。
④ 在第一層的兩瓣間，刻出第二層花瓣。
⑤ 繼續沿圓周挖除一圈，再刻花瓣。如此反覆數層即成花朵。
⑥ 將最外圈花瓣修成鋸齒狀。

① Cut off the stem end of a white radish. Use the thick end of the radish for this garnish. Trim one end to form a six-sided shape. (The side view should look like a trapezoid). One end should be narrower than the other.

② Make a cut behind each of the six sides; do not cut through. This will be the first row of petals.

③ Angle the knife to point away from the center of the radish; then diagonally insert it and cut along the rim of the radish. Cut off the excess radish; trim the rim to round out the sharp edge.

④ The second row of petals should be cut between the petals of the first row. Follow the procedure of cutting down on all six sides of the radish.

⑤ Cut the rim of the radish and round out the sharp edges as in Step ③ . Continue to cut the the rows of petals until the center is reached.

⑥ Cut out small v-shaped grooves around the edge of the first row of petals (outer petals). Soak the radish flower in water until ready for use. The water may be colored with food coloring.

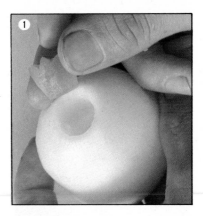

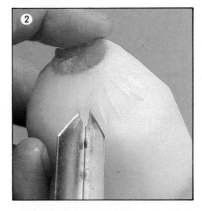

① 取白蘿蔔根部（或頭部）一段，頂端挖一凹洞，填入紅蘿蔔。

② 由頂端開始，雕細長花瓣。

③ 每雕出一層，就沿圓周切除一圈。

④ 全部雕好後，將底部略修整，經泡水或染色後使用。

① Cut off a 2 1/2 inch section (or desired length) from the stem end of a white radish. Cut off the stem; then pare the radish section. At the narrow end of the radish, hollow out a 1/2 inch hole in the center of the radish section. Fill the hole with a piece of carrot cut to the same size.

② Carve small v-shaped petals around the radish to form a geometric design.

③ Carve small petals around the radish; then cut out a small piece of radish from behind each row of petals. Continue to follow this step until the radish section is completely carved.

④ Cut off the uncarved part of the radish at the bottom; then slice across the base to remove the radish garnish. Soak the garnish flower in water until ready for use. The water may be colored with food coloring.

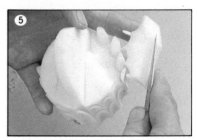

①取白蘿蔔根部（或頭部）一段，兩邊各切除一塊，成花籃狀。

②沿圓周挖除一圈小片，在同位置內側再刻一刀，刻出第一層花瓣。依同樣方法再刻出第二層花瓣。

③將籃把修圓。

④順籃把直刀往下切深。

⑤挖除籃中多餘部份。

⑥挖除籃把中央部份，並刻鋸齒花紋，即成花籃，中間插些小花及綠葉點綴。

① Cut off the stem end of a white radish. Use the thick end of the radish for this garnish. Make two cuts, approximately 1/2 inch apart, down 1 1/2 inches of the length of the radish. At the bottom of the 1 1/2 inches length, cut partially across on both sides of the 1/2 inch strip. This strip will serve as the handle of the basket. Remove both side sections.

② Carve around the bottom edge of radish to form indentations; remove the excess radish. Carve the first row of petals underneath the indentations already made. Carve the second row of petals behind the first row of petals.

③ Trim the square edges of the handle to form a semi-circle.

④ Starting at the bottom of the handle, slice off the excess radish of the second row of petals.

⑤ Remove the excess radish from both sides of the handle.

⑥ Carve out the center of the handle and remove the excess radish. Cut out small v-shaped grooves along the edges of the handle.

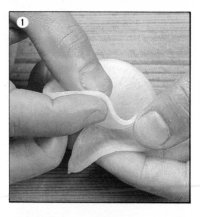

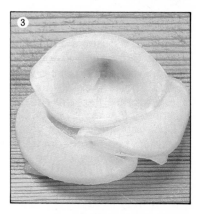

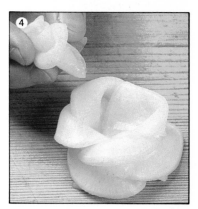

①白蘿蔔切圓薄片，共切八片。按水一杯加鹽一大匙的比例製成鹽水，將蘿蔔片浸泡鹽水使變軟。每片均用手撕開至圓心，再交疊成喇叭狀。

②從疊合處往外摺成爲花瓣。

③用三瓣交疊做底層。

④第二層用四瓣相互疊起，另取一片捲成螺旋狀做爲花心，插於中央即可。

① Cut off eight paper-thin, round slices from a white radish. The slices must be very thin. Soak the slices of radish in 1 cup of water and 1 Tbsp. salt for 20 minutes. The slices will become very soft and pliable. Cut each slice halfway across to the center. Gather the edges of the radish slice and curl the slice to a conical shape. Fold seven slices in this manner.

② Bend back half of the edge of each slice to resemble a flower petal.

③ Arrange three slices together, one on top of the other, as illustrated. This is the first layer of petals.

④ Separately place four more conical-shaped slices on top of the first layer with the seam arranged on different sides of the flower. Wrap the eighth slice by folding it around itself and placing it in the center.

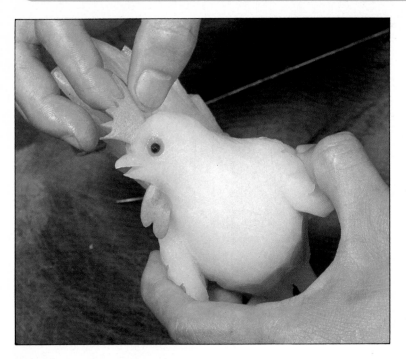

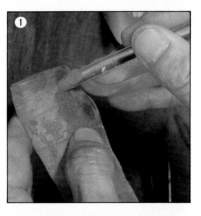

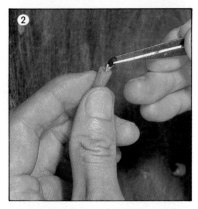

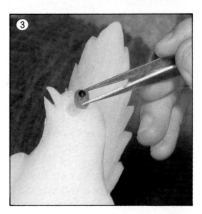

①用挖圓器挖取一小塊紅蘿蔔。

②將中心挖空插入火柴頭，做成雞眼。

③將做好的雞眼裝上。

④裝上用紅蘿蔔刻成的雞冠和肉垂。

① White radish is used for the body of the rooster. Carve out two small holes in a carrot. The carrot holes will be used for the eyes.

② Make a small hole in each carrot hole. Whiddle the top half of two matchsticks to a point and insert them into the little holes in the carrot holes. These will be the irises of the eyes.

③ Make a hole, the same size as the carrot hole, in the rooster's head where the eyes will be set. Carefully place the eyes in the holes.

④ Carve out the rooster's comb and wattle. Make two slits in the rooster's head to accommodate the comb and the wattle; slip the comb and wattle into the proper slits.

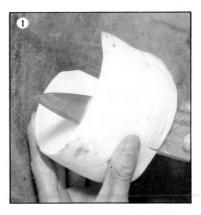

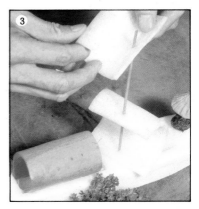

①取白蘿蔔中段，去皮。

②順著圓周片半圓筒狀薄片。

③將船身刻好，上置半圓筒紅蘿蔔當艙，二顆黑棗當身軀，戴上用紅蘿蔔和
大黃瓜刻成的斗笠點綴於船上。將細竹籤插於船中，再把切好的白蘿蔔插
上當帆。

④最後把紅櫻桃插在細竹籤上端即成。

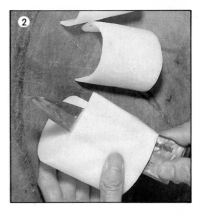

① Use the middle section of a white radish for this garnish. Pare the radish with a knife.

② Hold the cutting knife parallel to the radish; then cut three thin slices half way around the length of radish. The radish curls will be used as sails.

③ To arrange the details on the boat: Use two prunes for the bodies of the people. A piece of carrot and an end of a cucumber are used as hats. Lengthwise cut a thin slice of carrot half way around a carrot. The carrot curl will serve as the cabin. Use a piece of bamboo stick , or a skewer, as the mast. Pierce the three radish curls through the bamboo stick, as shown.

④ Top the mast with a maraschino cherry.

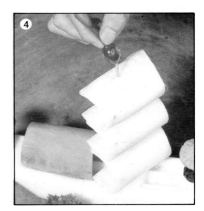

①白蘿蔔刻成船形，並在兩側刻魚鱗狀花紋，在船頭插上牙籤將刻好的龍頭裝上。

②裝上眼睛（參考第104頁）。將龍鬚裝在鼻翼處。

③在船的尾端將龍尾插上固定。

④黑棗串上牙籤插於龍船兩旁。

⑤再將櫻桃插於黑棗上。

⑥最後以小竹叉當槳插在船側。

① Use a white radish for the body of the boat. Score the sides of the radish in a crisscross fashion. Lengthwise hollow out two parallel rows along the center of the radish. Place toothpicks at one end of the radish to support the head of the dragon. Put the dragon's head in place.

② See page 104 for directions to make the eyes. Make two slits for the flames. Cut two thin strips of carrot to be used as the flames. Insert the carrot strips in the slits.

③ Put the dragon's tail in place; use toothpicks to attach the tail.

④ Insert toothpicks through the dates lengthwise and arrange them in the two shallow rows in the center of the radish.

⑤ Put maraschino cherries on the tips of the toothpicks on top of the Prunes.

⑥ Arrange cocktail forks on both sides of the dragon's body, as illustrated.

① 選粗大的白蘿蔔，切除兩側及根部，成長方條。
② 去皮後切出鵝的大約形態。
③ 再進一步修成鵝身。
④ 用火柴頭做眼睛，鵝頭前端插上牙籤套上一小段紅辣椒做鵝喙。
⑤ 鵝身兩側切除薄片成凹槽以裝翅。
⑥ 將刻好的鵝翅膀裝上即成。

① Select a long white radish for this garnish. Lengthwise cut off two
   sides of the radish. Cut off one end of the radish. The middle section
   of the radish is to be used for the body of the swan. Pare the radish
   with a knife.
② Roughly carve the body of the swan.
③ Carve the details of the body of the swan.
④ Use the tips of matchsticks for the eyes. Insert a toothpick in the head
   for the bill. Use pimento to form the bill.
⑤ Make two slits on the the sides of the body of the swan to
   accommodate the wings.
⑥ Slide the wings into the slits.

① 取紅蘿蔔頭部一段，在頂面刻一個小圓圈，並將小圓圈頂修圓。

② 沿小圓圈周圍斜刀挖除一圓片，使中央呈凹狀。

③ 沿小圓圈挖除數小片，在同位置後方再斜刻一刀，刻出第一層花瓣。

④ 在第一層花瓣下，橫刀切除一圈多餘部份，再刻第二層花瓣。如此反覆刻
數層即成花朵。將底部略修整，泡水後使用。

⑤⑥ 或在頂面挖除一星形，再依同樣方法刻出尖形花瓣。

① Cut off the stem end of a carrot. Use the thick end of a carrot for this garnish. At the thick end, carve around the center of the carrot to form a short post. Trim the post to make it round and smooth.

② Cut a thin slice around the carrot post; then remove the excess carrot circle.

③ Insert the cutting instrument slightly away from the post, pointing toward the base of the post. Make eight, evenly-spaced indentations around the post. Remove the excess pieces of carrot. Carve petals underneath each indentation. This is the first row of petals.

④ Continue to carve the petals around the carrot, alternating between the petals of the previous row. The petals take shape by carving out indentations then inserting the cutting instrument underneath the indentation. Continue to carve the petals until all the carrot is carved. Remove the carrot flower from the rest of the carrot by inserting the cutting instrument deep into the center and underneath each petal of the last row until the flower separates from the carrot. Soak the carrot flower in water until ready for use. OR

⑤⑥ Carve an eleven-pointed star in the center of the thick end of a carrot. Follow Steps ① - ④ but cut 'v' shaped petals.

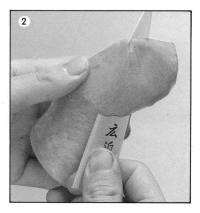

① 取紅蘿蔔一段，頂端修成錐形。
② 順錐形片薄片。
③ 片2—3圈。
④ 邊緣刻鋸齒狀，泡水後使用。可另製小花擺在中央點綴。

① Cut off a section of carrot and trim the tip to a point.
② Diagonally slice a continuous, thin slice around the pointed end of the carrot.
③ Continue slicing around the pointed end of the carrot until there are two or three complete circles. Remove the curl on the final turn.
④ Carve v-shaped grooves around the outer edge of the carrot slice. Soak the carrot slice in water until ready for use. Another smaller flower may be placed in the center of this garnish.

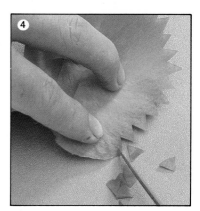

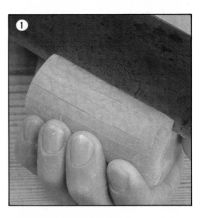

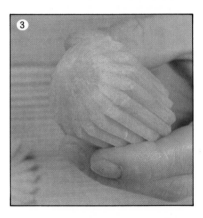

①取紅蘿蔔一段，修成圓筒狀，在圓周面每隔0.7公分刻1公分深的直條紋。
②在直條紋兩邊，交叉斜切，修成波浪形。
③頂端修成錐形。
④順錐形片2－3圈薄片，捲成花朵狀，泡水後使用。

① Pare a carrot and trim it to make the surface smooth and round. Cut 1/2 inch deep, v-shaped grooves every 1/3 inch around the length of the carrot.
② Remove the long v-shaped pieces of excess carrot.
③ Trim one end of the carrot to a point.
④ Carefully cut a continuous, thin slice around the pointed end of the carrot in a circular fashion until two or three complete circles have been carved. Remove the curl on the final turn. Bend the ends in toward each other to produce two conical shapes. Soak the carrot in water until ready for use.

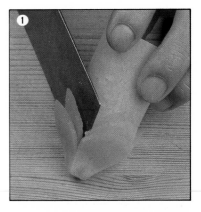

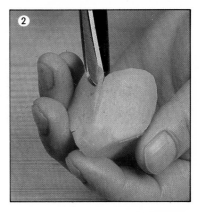

①取紅蘿蔔一段，修成圓筒狀（直徑約3公分）。頂端修成四角錐形，順著四角錐深切兩層，內層要切斷，並用手輕輕拽開。

②兩瓣間用剪刀修整齊。

③由底部插入細竹籤。

④將內層四片花瓣插在竹籤上固定，泡水即展開成花朵。將細竹籤往下拉，再套上香菜莖（或巴西利）做花莖。

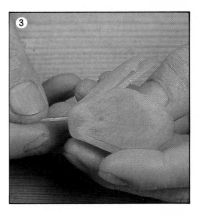

① Peel the carrot and trim the surface to make it smooth and round. Diagonally cut one end to a square. Make a deep cut (petal) behind each flat surface; do not cut through. Cut a second row of petals behind the first row; cut through. Twist the end of the flower and pull it off.

② Use scissors to cut a v-shaped wedge between the petals.

③ Starting at the base of the petals, insert a toothpick into the center of the flower.

④ Gather the tips of the second row of petals; pierce the tips through the toothpick. Soak the garnish in water until ready for use. Carefully pull the toothpick down below the surface of the blossom to conceal it. Use a piece of parsley sprig or coriander stem to cover **exposed end of the toothpick.**

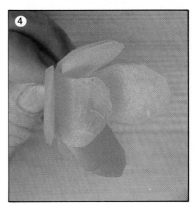

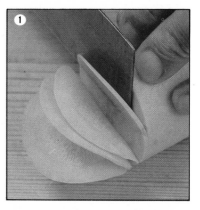

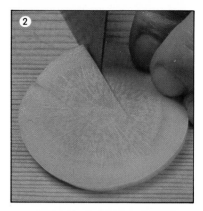

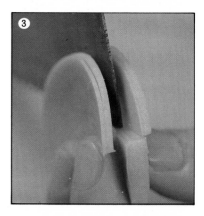

① 取紅蘿蔔一段，修成圓筒狀，片切 0.1 公分薄片，底端留 1/2 不切斷，共切四片。

② 在底端相連處切兩刀呈八形。

③ 在每兩片間切斷，成二片一組共二組。

④ 一手捏住底端，另一手提起一端插在底中央，另一端亦插上，泡水後使用。

① Pare a carrot and trim it to smooth its surface to a round shape. Cut three paper-thin slices to within 1/2 inch of the bottom. (The slices should be connected at the bottom). On the fourth slice, cut through.

② On the connected edge, make two cuts slanting inward (八), cut past the center of the slices.

③ Hold the sliced carrot so that there are two slices on each side of your fingers; separate the center slightly, stopping just short of the cuts made in Step ② . Repeat this procedure for the other cut side.

④ Hold the connected edge (it will serve as the pedestal or foot). Push up half of the sliced section so that it will "fan" out; push in the bottom slightly so that the joined edge will rest securely on itself (on the pedestal). Repeat this procedure for the opposite side (slices). Turn the carrot section and repeat the process twice on the other side (other slices) to form the shape that is illustrated. Soak the garnish in water until ready for use.

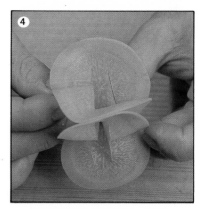

① 取紅蘿蔔一段（長約10公分），去皮，縱剖兩半，切片不切到底（可在兩旁墊兩隻筷子較易切）。
② 在圓面刻五條直溝。
③ 在背面切斜刀，不切到底。
④ 彎曲兩端（圓面朝外），用牙籤固定之，泡水後使用。

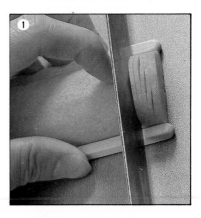

① Pare a carrot. Cut a three inches section in half lengthwise. Turn the carrot half curve side up, then place a chopstick on both sides of the carrot lengthwise. Thinly slice across the length of the carrot half; stop at the chopsticks.

② Cut five, evenly-spaced, v-shaped grooves down the length of the carrot. Remove the excess carrot.

③ Turn the carrot half, flat side up. Diagonally cut paper-thin slices to about 1/4 inch from the bottom

④ Turn the carrot curve side up. Gather together the ends of the carrot, curve side out; then join the ends with two toothpick halves. Soak the garnish in water until ready for use.

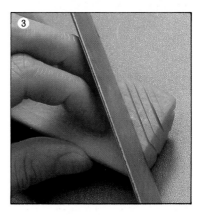

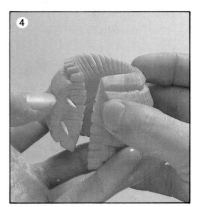

① 取紅蘿蔔一段，修成圓筒狀，在頂面刻星狀做記號。
② 以星形各尖端爲準，在圓周面刻 1 公分深之直條紋。
③ 斜刀切除直條紋兩側多餘部份，並修圓成梅花形。
④ 在瓣尖上交叉斜切∨形切口。
⑤ 順∨形切口向兩側分別切開一缺口。
⑥ 頂端修成錐形，順錐形片 2－3 圈薄片，捲成花朵，泡水後使用。

① Pare the carrot and trim it to smooth its surface to a round shape. Outline a star in the center of the thick end of the carrot.
② The cuts made in Steps ② - ⑤ should extend down the length of the carrot. Cut out a 1/2 inch deep, v-shaped groove at each point of the star (extend the cut down the length of the carrot).
③ Remove the v-shaped wedges from the length and trim the points to round them out.
④ Cut out a v-shaped groove at each rounded tip of the star.
⑤ On each side of the rounded tips of the star, cut two thin petals.
⑥ Trim the end of the carrot to a point. Carefully slice a thin, continuous slice in a circular fashion, until two or three complete circles have been carved. Remove the carrot curl on the final turn. Bend the ends in toward each other to produce two conical shapes. The curl will hold the conical shapes in place.

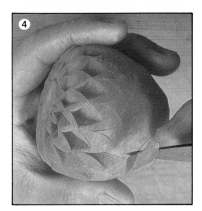

①取紅蘿蔔頭部一段，頂端修圓。
②在中心先刻除一條細圓圈。
③沿圓圈斜刀交切刻除∨形花紋共16個，在同位置外側再斜刀交切刻一圈，
　刻出第一層花瓣。在兩瓣間再斜刀交切剔出菱形塊。（圖示是以尖刀來
　刻，亦可用尖形雕刻刀來做）。
④依同樣方法，全部刻好，泡水後使用。

① Pare a carrot; then cut off a section from the stem end. Trim the carrot section so that it is wide across the top and narrow toward the bottom. Round off the top end. Use a knife with a sharp point or the "v"-shaped blade carving tool.

② Carve then remove a circular grove around the center of the stem end to serve as a guide for carving other grooves. Mark off four evenly-spaced points around the top of the carrot. Carve out four V-shaped grooves at these points. Carve three more evenly-spaced grooves between the first and second sections. Carve three evenly-spaced grooves between each of the remaining sections. There should be sixteen v-shaped grooves on the top of the carrot when finished.

③ Outline the v-shape using the first row as a guide. Carve out elongated diamond-shapes between the first carvings. Continue carving diamond-shaped sections between the first carvings.

④ Use the previous row as a guide then continue to carve out diamond-shaped sections until the carrot has been completely carved. Soak the garnish in water until ready for use.

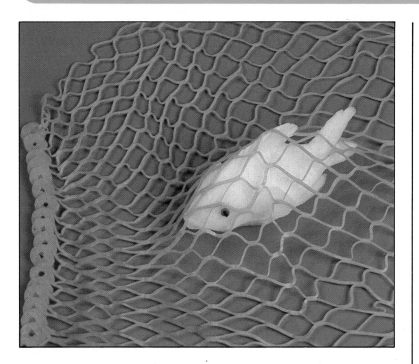

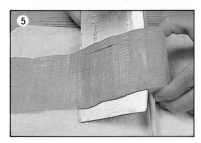

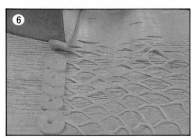

① 取紅蘿蔔一段修成四方柱。將筷子修尖旋轉插入紅蘿蔔中央。

② 抽出筷子，將紅蘿蔔泡入鹽水中（水 2 杯加鹽 2 大匙）泡約 4 小時，泡軟後較易切。

③ 循原洞插上筷子，先上、下各切一刀（觸及筷子），相隔0.5公分處再由左、右各切一刀，如此反覆上下、左右全部切好（兩刀相隔的距離愈小，切出的網愈細）。

④ 拭乾蘿蔔上的水份（泡軟的蘿蔔易出水），用手挾緊，由四方修成圓筒形。

⑤ 旋轉片成厚薄一致的長條薄片。

⑥ 取出筷子，順網紋切斷心部，攤開成魚網狀，覆蓋在菜餚上。

① Lengthwise cut a thick carrot to a long rectangular shape. Plunge a wooden or steel skewer lengthwise through the center of the carrot.

② Remove the skewer and place the carrot in 2 cups of water and 2 Tbsp. salt. Soak the carrot for 4 hours. (The soaking will soften the carrot and make it easier to cut.)

③ Re-insert the skewer into the carrot. Mentally number the sides of the carrot. Opposite sides will be cut the same way (sides 1 and 3 will be cut the same way; sides 2 and 4 will be cut the same way). Starting on side one, 1/4 inch from the end of the carrot, cut the carrot down to the skewer. Turn the carrot to side 3, cut 1/4 inch from the end down to the skewer. Turn the carrot to side 2, cut 1/2 inch from the edge. Turn the carrot to side 4; cut down 1/2 inch from the edge. Continue to cut the opposite sides in the order specified.

④ Remove the skewer and place the carrot in 2 cups of water and 2 carrot together to remove as much water as possible. Re-insert the skewer through the carrot and squeeze it together. Trim the sharp edges of the carrot to make it round.

⑤ Hold the cutting knife parallel to the carrot. Cut a long continuous slice around the length of the carrot.

⑥ Remove the skewer; cut the carrot between the first cut made in order to separate and unfold the net. Arrange this garnish over prepared dishes to resemble a fish net.

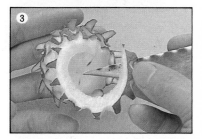

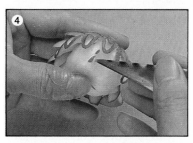

① 沿小紅蘿蔔底邊雕一圈花瓣，同位置內側再雕第二層花瓣。
② 頂部切除一片。
③ 斜刀沿圓周挖除一圈。
④ 將圓周略修圓。
⑤ 繼續雕第三層花瓣，如此反覆雕數層即成花朵，泡水後使用。
⑥ 或僅刻出兩層花瓣，保留頂端的綠莖。

① Carve petals around the non stem end of the radish. This will be the first row of petals. Carve a second row of petals behind the first row of petals.
② Slice off the stem end of the radish.
③ Cut and remove the rim around the white center of the radish.
④ Trim the white part of the radish to make it smooth.
⑤ Continue carving petals for the third and subsequent rows until the whole radish has been carved. Place the flower radish in water until ready for use. OR
⑥ Carve only two rows of petals and leave the stem intact.

① 沿小紅蘿蔔底邊先切除五片。同位置內側再刻一刀，刻出第一層花瓣。每兩瓣間再切除一片。

② 同位置內側再刻一刀，即刻出第二層花瓣，同樣方法繼續刻出第三層或第四層花瓣。

③ 片除頂面紅皮。

④ 略修整齊，泡水後使用。

⑤ 或刻出二層花瓣，沿圓周挖除一圈並略修圓，頂端刻六角星形。

⑥ 或僅刻出一層花瓣，沿圓周挖除一圈並略修圓，頂端直刀交切成方格紋。

① Slice off five evenly-spaced, thin, circular pieces around the non stem end of a radish. Carve five petals behind the five flat surfaces left by the previous cuts; do not cut through. This will be the first row of petals. Carve out and remove the red skin of radish between the petals of the first row.

② Carve the second row of petals behind and between the petals of the first row. Continue to carve petals, alternately, as before; remove excess radish; continue to carve petals until several rows have been carved.

③ Cut off the non stem end of the radish.

④ Trim to smooth the center of the radish. Soak the flower radish in water until ready for use. OR

⑤ Carve out two rows of petals and trim the sides. Carve out a star on top of the radish. OR

⑥ Carve only one row of petals and trim the sides. Score the top in a crisscross fashion.

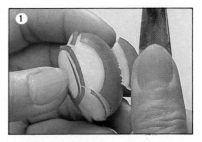

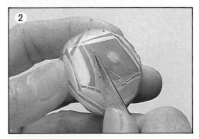

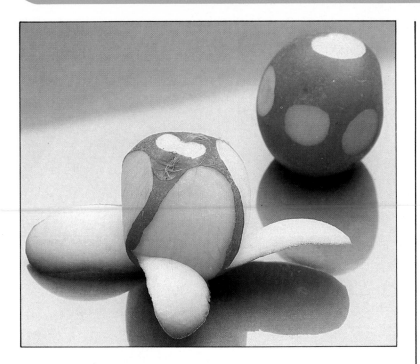

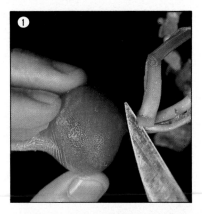

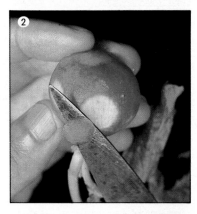

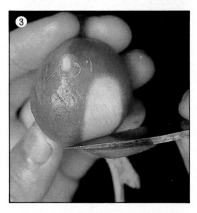

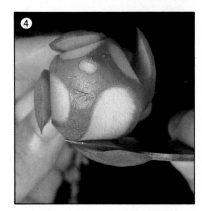

①切除部份老葉。
②切去根，在圓周等距切除4小片小圓皮。
③由根部斜切0.1公分之薄皮切至頂端，不切斷。
④共切四片，泡水後薄皮即展開成花朵狀。

① Remove some of the leaves from the radish and trim the root.
② Cut off four evenly-spaced circular pieces around the radish. Slice off a small piece from the non stem end of the radish.
③ Slice down along the length of the radish from the stem end to the non stem end without cutting through. Twist the knife slightly to make a petal shape.
④ Cut paper-thin slices to total four petals around the radish. Soak the radish in water until ready for use.

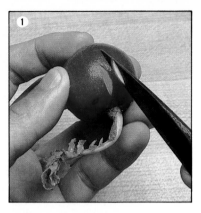

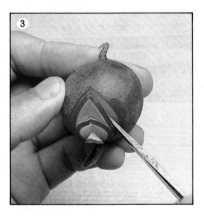

①沿小紅蘿蔔周圍斜刀交切刻除月牙形小塊，等距離共切除四小塊。
②在月牙缺口兩側，分別斜刀切入，兩刀相交於中央，即刻出第一層花瓣，
　花瓣兩旁再各切除一小片，使第一層花瓣更明顯。
③依同樣方法，繼續刻出第二及第三層花瓣。
④頂端斜刀深切四刀成菱形，去除頂端並略修齊即成。

①Make four small evenly-spaced, v-shaped cuts around the length of a radish close to the stem. Remove excess radish to leave a groove.
②Make a cut on both sides of the v-shaped groove—the cuts should be deep enough to meet. Remove a thin piece of radish from both sides of this petal.
③Follow Step ② to make two more rows of petals and to complete the other three v-shaped grooves.
④On the non stem end make deep cuts toward the center to form a diamond-shaped indentations; remove the excess radish. Soak the radish in water until ready for use.

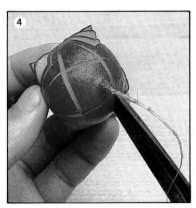

可取材甜菜莖、蘿蔔莖或其他蔬菜莖。
①將有葉的部份切去，僅使用莖。
②在莖上斜刀劃鱗片狀。
③較粗的莖剖開爲二或三條。
④泡在水中即展開並捲曲非常美觀，將底修平即可平放擺飾。

Use the stem of a beet or the stem of a white radish for this garnish.
①Remove most of the green leafy portion of the stem. Slice off a piece of beet with the stem so that it will sit flat.
②Make diagonal cuts along the length of each stem, being careful not to cut through to the bottom of the stem.
③Cut the thick stem lengthwise into two or three strips.
④Soak the garnish in water. The stem strips will curl up and "blossom".

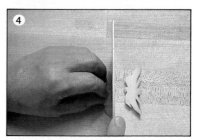

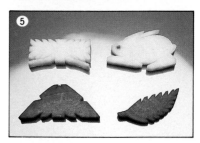

① 將西洋芹菜花的部份切下，留做他用。
② 莖去皮，修成長方塊。
③ 在四邊適當位置切除小三角塊如圖。
④ 切片即成蝴蝶狀。
⑤⑥ 亦可用其他不同的材料，刻出各種不同花樣的平面盤飾。

① Remove the floweretts and their small branches from the stem of broccoli.
② Cut off the skin from the stem of broccoli. Cut a section of the stem into a cube shape.
③ Carve out several triangular-shaped pieces to form the shape of a butterfly.
④ Turn the cube shape so that the cuts face horizontally. Slice across the butterfly-shaped stem to remove individual butterfly shapes. OR
⑤ ⑥ You may use other kinds of vegetables to cut a variety of shapes.

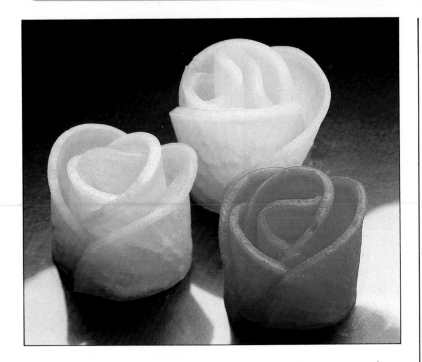

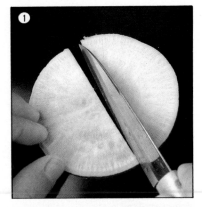

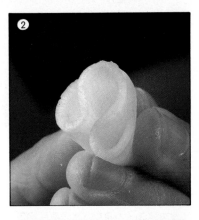

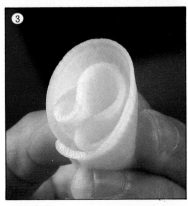

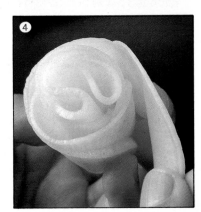

①蘿蔔切半圓形薄片，用鹽水泡軟。

②取一張蘿蔔片，先對摺，再將兩端分別向外反摺，做爲花心。

③再取一張包裹在花心上。

④如此繼續將半圓片包裹上即成花形。一朵花共需五張半圓片。

① Cut a white radish into thin slices. Cut each slice in half. Soak the radish halves in salted water. (The salt water will soften the radish slices and make them pliable).

② Take one half slice of radish and fold it in half; place the flat side down. Bend back the ends (opposite the first fold) so that the half slice resembles an accordion fold (fan). This will be the center of the flower.

③ Hold the center petal in your hand and arrange four half slices around the center petal.

④ One flower consists of five half slices of radish.

①火腿切成長方形薄片，共切32片。

②取一片捲成花心。

③每片均摺成直角⤵，摺角處向上，一層層包捲在花心上。

④用牙籤固定底部即成。

⑤除火腿外，亦可用紅蘿蔔或白蘿蔔來做。

⑥或用蛋黃做成蛋黃餅，再切片來做。

　蛋黃餅做法：蛋黃17個，依序加入鹽半小匙、太白粉 2 大匙、水 2 大匙，
　拌勻並過濾後倒入 7 公分×14公分鋁製容器內（其他容器亦可，厚度有2.5
　公分以上為理想），容器內需先鋪玻璃紙，水開後大火蒸約20分鐘至熟。

① Slice cooked ham into 32 rectangular pieces.

② Take one slice of ham and roll it like a jelly roll to form the center of the flower.

③ Fold the rectangular slices in half to form an angle ⤵. While holding the center petal in your hand, take another folded slice and place it around the center petal. The folded edge will form the top of the petal. Continue placing the petals around the previously arranged petals until all (31) folded slices have been put in place.

④ Insert a toothpick through the bottom of the flower to hold the petals in place.

⑤ White radish and a carrot were used to prepare this garnish.

⑥ Slices of Egg Yolk Cake are used to prepare this garnish.

To prepare Egg Yolk Cake:

Lightly beat 17 egg yolks. Add, in this order, then beat after each addition: 1/2 tsp. salt, 2 Tbsp. cornstarch, and 2 Tbsp. water. Use a container lined with wax paper that is 2 3/4 inches wide by 5 1/2 inches long and more than 1 inch deep. Pour the mixture through a sieve into the container. Place the container in a double boiler and steam the egg yolk mixture for 20 minutes.

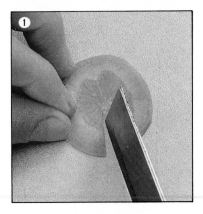

① 切 5 張圓薄片，每張由圓心向外切開一缺口。

② 切口相疊插在牙籤上。

③ 一張張交錯串成花朵，隨意取材做花心，泡水後使用。

④ 可用多種不同材料來做，例如：小紅蘿蔔、黃瓜、白蘿蔔、茄子等。

① Cut five paper-thin slices from a carrot. Cut half way through each slice from the center out.

② Overlap the pointed edges of the carrot slice. Hold the ends together by piercing them with a toothpick.

③ Follow Step ③ for each slice. Arrange the conical-shaped slices in a circular fashion by inserting each carrot slice through the toothpick; arrange them seam side down. Cover the tip of the toothpick with your favorite topping (green pea, corn kernel, white or green onion, red pepper, or a cross section of the stem of a green vegetable). Soak the garnish in water until ready for use.

④ Many kinds of vegetables may be used for this garnish, for example, radish, cucumber, white radish, and eggplant.

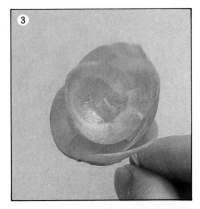

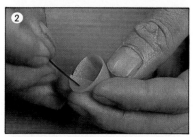

① 蘿蔔片切四種不同大小的缺口，（切除 $\frac{1}{2}$、$\frac{1}{3}$、$\frac{1}{4}$ 及切縫），每種三片爲一組。

② 由面積最小的一組開始，切口相疊用細竹籤由上往下串。

③ 三片串好，相疊一起成立體三角形。

④⑤ 次小的依序串上。依此類推全部串好。

⑥ 將竹籤輕輕往下拉，用香菜莖套上做花莖，泡水後使用。

① Pare a carrot and trim it to make it round and smooth. Cut twelve paper-thin slices (The slices must be paper thin.) Cut three circles in half. Cut out one third from three other slices. Cut out one-quarter from three slices. Cut half way through, from the center out of the remaining three slices, (   ).

② Overlap the pointed ends of the half circles to form a conical shape. Hold the ends together by piercing them with a toothpick. Gather the two other half circles and pierce the ends with a toothpick to hold them in place; arrange them seam side down.

③ Arrange the conical shape so that the three pointed tips form a triangle.

④⑤ Gather the pointed edges of the two-thirds circles and overlap them to form a conical shape; place them over the first conical shapes. Pierce the ends with the toothpick and arrange the tips to form a triangle. Continue forming the three-fourth circles and whole circles into conical shapes and arranging them as bofore.

⑥ Carefully slide the toothpick down below the surface of the rose to conceal it. Use a parsley sprig or coriander stem to cover the exposed end of the toothpick. Place the garnish in water until ready for use.

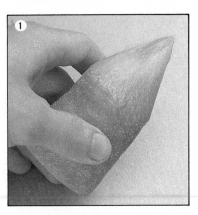

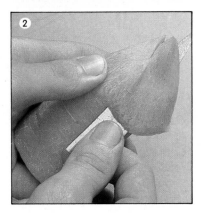

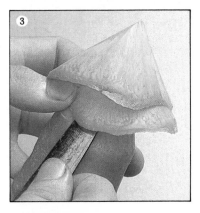

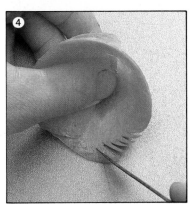

①將紅蘿蔔一端修成圓錐形。

②順圓錐片薄片。

③需片1⅓圈。

④在邊緣修鋸齒形。依同法再刻白蘿蔔，將紅、白蘿蔔套在一起，泡水後使用。中央可擺上小紅蘿蔔花點綴。

① Use the middle section of a carrot. Trim one end to a point.

② Carefully slice a continuous thin slice, in a circular fashion, around the pointed end of a carrot.

③ Continue slicing, in a circular fashion, around the pointed end until one and one-third turns have been completed. Remove carrot curl on the last turn.

④ Carve v-shaped grooves around the edge of the carrot slice. Use the same procedure to carve a white radish. Place the carved carrot section in the center of the carved white radish section. Soak the garnish in water until ready for use. A carved radish may be placed in the center of this garnish.

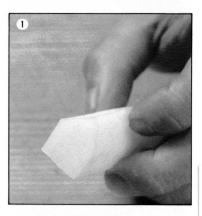

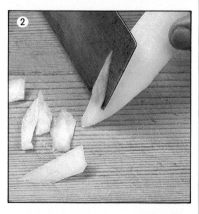

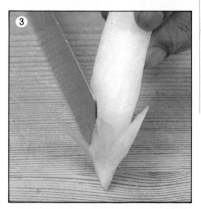

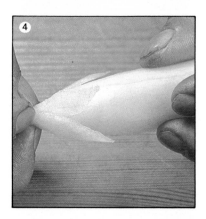

① 將蘿蔔切成五角柱（四角亦可），直徑約2.5公分。
② 順五個面修成錐形。
③ 由每面向下斜切，刀尖切至頂端，不切斷，共切五瓣。
④ 用手輕輕捜動取下花朵，泡水後使用，亦可染色使用。

① Pare a white radish or carrot. Lengthwise cut it into a five-sided shape, as illustrated.
② Trim one end to a point.
③ Diagonally place the blade of the knife behind the flat surface to cut down toward the point. Make a cut into the corner of each of the five sides; stop just short of the bottom to form petals.
④ Twist the end of the flower stem and pull if off. Place the garnish in water and let it soak until ready for use. Food coloring may be added to the water.

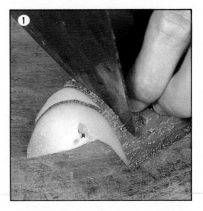

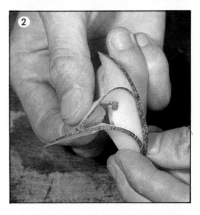

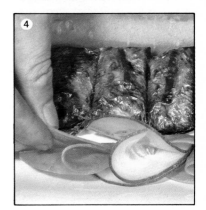

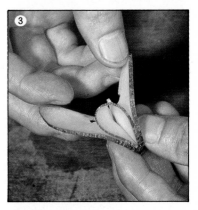

①大黃瓜縱切兩半，去頭，切片，第一、二刀不切斷，第三刀切斷，三片爲一組。
②將中間一片彎曲。
③內摺。
④黃瓜、紅蘿蔔相間，排飾於盤邊。

①Cut a cucumber in half lengthwise. Cut and remove the stem end; discard. Make three, paper-thin slices, do not cut through the first two slices; cut through the third slice. The three slices will be joined as a set.
②Fold the middle slice toward the center.
③Insert the middle slice securely to hold it in place.
④A carrot may be used for this garnish and arranged alternately with a cucumber, as illustrated.

①先將生菜、巴西利鋪盤上墊底，把做好的花籃置其上（番茄做的花籃內
　裝小花點綴，參考第72頁）。
②小黃瓜切細條做葉莖，櫻桃片及小青豆做花蕾。
③切兩片番茄薄皮，並切直條紋，一端不切斷，擺飾兩邊。
④配上黃瓜葉即成。
　黃瓜葉做法：黃瓜縱切取約 0.5 公分厚之半圓，切薄片，第一刀不切斷，
　第二刀切斷，二片打開即成。

① Place a lettuce leaf and parsley sprigs in the center of a dish.
   Arrange the tomato garnish (see page 72) on the parsley sprigs.
② Make long thin leaves by cutting strips from the skin of a cucumber.
   Cut off a small section from the non stem end of a maraschino
   cherry. Place the section of cherry at the tip of the thin leaves; set a
   cooked pea on top of the cherry to resemble a "flower bud".
③ Cut two paper-thin slices of tomato, both slices must have skin on
   one side. Make several thin slices; turn them skin side up, do not cut
   through. Place one of the tomato pieces on each side of the
   tomato garnish. Carefully separate the tomato strips slightly.
④ Cut a 1/4 inch thick strip from the length of a cucumber; the strip
   must have skin on one side. Turn the cucumber strip flat side down;
   make a paper-thin slice, do not cut through; make another paper-
   thin slice, cut through. The two slices will be joined as a set. Carefully
   open the slices to resemble a leaf. Place the cucumber leaves near
   the tomato garnish.

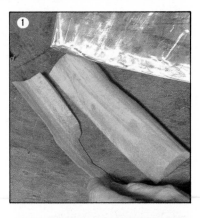

①紅蘿蔔修成15公分長半圓形。

②半圓面上刻6－7條直溝。

③在圓面切薄片深至⅘處，放入鹽水內浸泡約３小時至軟。

④用手及刀面推壓成扇形，同樣方法刻好黃瓜，再將紅蘿蔔疊上即可。

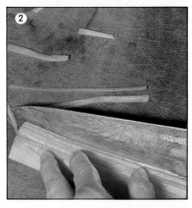

①Pare a six-inch carrot. Cut the carrot lengthwise in half. Trim the carrot to make it smooth. Place the carrot flat side down.

②Cut six or seven v-shaped long grooves along the length of the carrot; remove excess carrot wedges.

③Slice the carrot thinly crosswise to 1/5 from the opposite side. Soak the carrot piece in salted water for three hours; the carrot will become very pliable.

④Use the flat edge of a cleaver to gently flatten the carrot to resemble a "fan". Follow Steps ① - ④ to prepare a cucumber. Place the carrot on top of the cucumber, as illustrated.

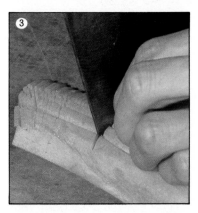

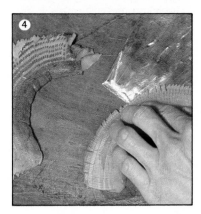

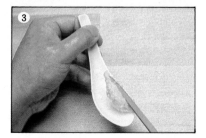

①做金魚燕窩需準備以下材料

湯匙	青豆	燕窩	雞絨
紅蘿蔔片	黃瓜	豬油	紅色雞絨（雞絨內加紅蘿蔔）
筍片	冬菇絲		

②在湯匙上塗一層油。

③將雞絨填在湯匙上並抹平。

④用筍片做背鰭，紅蘿蔔做魚尾，各放在適當位置。

⑤用小黃瓜做腹鰭，將燕窩鋪滿魚身，再用紅色雞絨做出魚頭形狀。

⑥加香菇絲在頭部做點綴，用青豆做眼睛。放入蒸籠內蒸 5 分鐘即成。

①The following ingredients and materials are used to prepare the garnish in this photograph:

Chinese soup spoon   Peas

Slices of carrot   Cucumber slices

Slices of canned bamboo shoots   Strips of black mushroom

Bird's nest ·

Lard (oil or other substitutes may be used to prevent sticking)

Chicken meat paste (mix with a little cornstarch)

Red chicken meat paste (Finely chopped carrot is added to the chicken meat to make it "red".)

②Lightly grease the inside of a soup spoon.

③Place the Chicken meat paste in the spoon and level it off.

④Use bamboo shoot slices to make the dorsal fin of the fish and the carrot slices to make the tail fin.

⑤Cucumber slices are used to make the ventral fin. Place some of the bird's nest on top of the chicken meat paste to form the body of the fish. The red chicken paste is used to make the head of the fish.

⑥Place the strips of black mushroom to indicate the separation between the head and body of the fish. A pea is used for the eye. Place the spoon in a steamer and cook for 5 minutes. Carefully remove the fish garnish from the spoon and use as desired.

Dried and cleaned birds' nests may be purchased at a Chinese drug store. Soak the bird's nest in water, until soft, before using it.

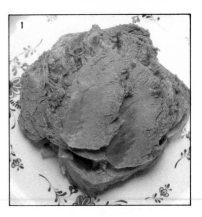

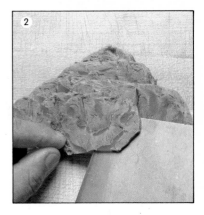

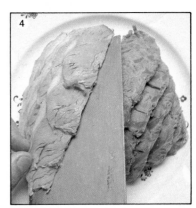

① 牛肉切片,將碎片先堆在盤中央,留30片完整的用來覆蓋其上。
② 將牛肉排成上窄下寬的塔形,共用15片。
③ 將排好的牛肉片用刀面劃起,整齊的放在牛肉碎片的一邊。
④ 同樣方法再用15片牛肉,排出另一個塔形,放在盤子的另一邊,中央以小黃瓜片(16片)點綴。此盤為單拼。

① Cut cooked rolled rump roast into thin slices. Select 30 whole slices. Place the remaining slices in a mound in the center of a plate.

② Take 15 slices of roast and arrange them in a triangular shape with slices overlapping, as shown.

③ Use the flat side of a cleaver to lift the 15 slices; place them on top and to one side of the beef already on the dish.

④ Follow the same procedure given in Steps ② - ③ for the remaining 15 slices but place them on the other side to completely cover the center. Place 16 slices of cucumber, slightly overlapping, to cover the inside edges (seam) of the slices of meat.

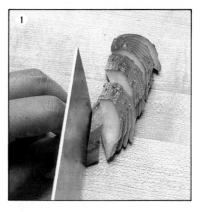

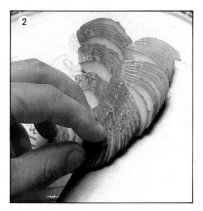

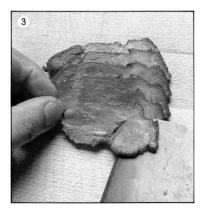

①小黃瓜縱剖兩半,每半切斜片,每七片一組(一邊不切斷)。

②排在長盤中央。

③叉燒切片,並將邊緣略修齊排在最左邊。

④選較方整的肉片緊接着放在上面。另一邊用其他材料按同樣方法排好,此 為雙拼。

①Cut a cucumber in half lengthwise. Cut seven paper-thin slices but do not cut through; cut through the eighth slice. The entire length of the cucumber half is to be cut in this manner.

②Use the flat side of a cleaver to lift the sliced cucumber and to place it in the center of a serving platter.

③Cut thin slices of roast (pork roast is shown). Arrange the sliced meat by overlapping the slices as shown. Trim the short edges of the sliced meat.

④Place the slices of roast on one side of the platter. The other slices of roast are cut and arrange in the same manner and placed on top of the cucumber slices. Slices of abalone are shown in this photograph; however, other kinds of meat may be used.

① 叉燒切長方薄片，共切14片，疊排成略呈弧形的長條，並將邊緣修齊。

② 用刀面剷起排在盤邊。

③ 採用七種材料，按叉燒、鮑魚、火腿、冬菇、蛋黃、五香牛肉、小黃瓜順序排好。

④ 番茄切半圓形薄片，在內圈整齊的排一圈。

⑤ 中間空位裝入海蜇皮。

⑥ 其上再排鹽水蝦及糖醋排骨。此盤為大拼。

① Cut 14 thin slices of cooked pork roast. Sightly fan out the slices and trim the edges.

② Use the flat side a cleaver to lift the slices of pork and to arrange them along the side of a serving platter.

③ Use six other kinds of meats or ingredients of your preference. The photographs shows (clockwise): sliced pork, cucumber, beef, egg yolk cake, black mushroom, cooked ham, and abalone.

④ Arrange sliced tomato halves overlapping them around the center of the platter, as shown.

⑤ Place cooked jellyfish or another cooked ingredient in the center of the platter.

⑥ Arrange cooked salted shrimp, sweet and sour short ribs on top and to one side of the jellyfish.

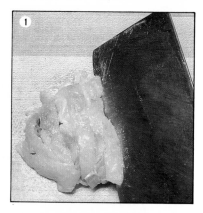

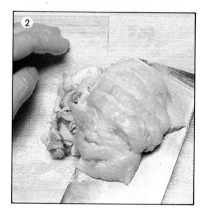

①將雞塊略修整齊，切下的邊角及較碎的肉先切小塊堆一邊。再將雞塊剁成長方塊。

②將整齊的肉塊蓋在碎塊上，並用手拱起成半圓形。

③用刀面剷起。

④放在大盤上。使用五種不同材料，照上法堆排成梅花形，在空隙擺些盤飾即成"五福拼盤"。

① Use a cooked (boiled) chicken breast for this platter. Trim the chicken breast to obtain a neat bulk. Set aside the pieces of meat that have been trimmed off. Cut the chicken breast into strips.

② Gather together the pieces of chicken breast that were trimmed off. Use the flat side of a cleaver to carefully pick up the pieces of chicken. Place the strips of chicken over the pieces that were trimmed off. Use your hands to mold and pack the chicken together.

③ Use the flat side of a cleaver to lift the packed chicken meat.

④ Carefully set it on a serving platter. An assortment of four other ingredients are arranged on the platter to resemble a plum blossom.

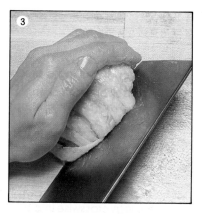

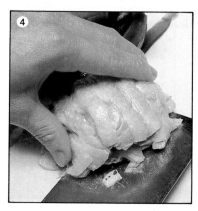

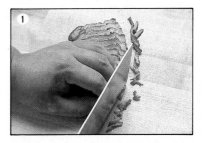

① 叉燒切長方薄片，共切14片，疊排成略呈弧形的長條，並將邊緣修齊。

② 用刀面剷起排在盤邊。

③ 採用七種材料，按叉燒、鮑魚、火腿、冬菇、蛋黃、五香牛肉、小黃瓜順序排好。

④ 番茄切半圓形薄片，在內圈整齊的排一圈。

⑤ 中間空位裝入海蜇皮。

⑥ 其上再排鹽水蝦及糖醋排骨。此盤為大拼。

① Cut 14 thin slices of cooked pork roast. Sightly fan out the slices and trim the edges.

② Use the flat side a cleaver to lift the slices of pork and to arrange them along the side of a serving platter.

③ Use six other kinds of meats or ingredients of your preference. The photographs shows (clockwise): sliced pork, cucumber, beef, egg yolk cake, black mushroom, cooked ham, and abalone.

④ Arrange sliced tomato halves overlapping them around the center of the platter, as shown.

⑤ Place cooked jellyfish or another cooked ingredient in the center of the platter.

⑥ Arrange cooked salted shrimp, sweet and sour short ribs on top and to one side of the jellyfish.

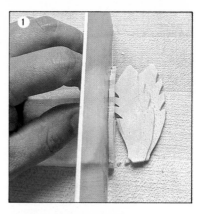

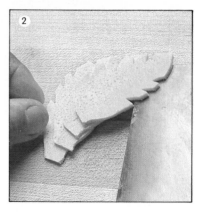

① 將蛋黃餅（做法參考第128頁）修成葉形，切17或19片。

②③④將蛋黃片，一片片排成花瓣形（尖或圓瓣均可）。也可中央先放一片，再左右交疊排列（如大圖片所示）。

使用不同的材料做其他花瓣，需注意顏色的調配。外圈的花瓣排好後再排內圈，先用黃瓜片排一圈，再用番茄片排一圈。中央擺飾一些花朵即成。

① Cut out wedges along the sides of a rectangular-shaped egg yolk cake. (The cross section should resemble a leaf). Slice the cake crosswise into 17 or 19 sliecs.

②③④ Arrange the egg yolk cake slices to form a leaf pattern or arrange them as shown in the large photograph by placing a slice on both sides of the first slice then alternating sides and overlapping the rest of the slices.

Other ingredients may be used to prepare the other petals, as shown. Outer petals are placed first then the inside petals are arranged between and slightly overlapping the first (outer) layer. Halved cucumber slices are arranged, slightly overlapping, in a circle over the second row of petals. Halved tomato are placed, overlapping, over the cucumber slices. The center is decorated with various kinds of flowers and Chinese parsley (cilantro).

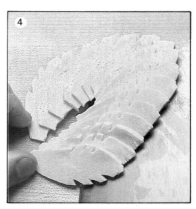

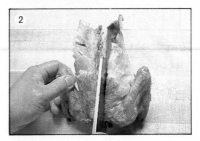

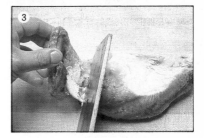

雞的剁法：

① 先在雞背上劃十字刀痕，再切下二隻雞腿。

② 雞身由中央剁開爲兩半，再剁去雞背脊骨。

③ 除下雞翼。

④ 將雞胸剁塊，置大盤中央。

⑤ 雞腿剁塊，排放在兩旁。

⑥ 將雞翼放在靠頂處即成。

Steps to follow in cutting a precooked chicken:

① On the back of the chicken, close to the neck, score a cross. Turn the chicken over (breast side up). Cut off the legs at the top (thigh) joint.

② Cut the chicken in half lengthwise. Turn the chicken over (breast side down) and cut out the spine. Turn the chicken breast side up.

③ Cut off the wings.

④ Cut the chicken crosswise into slices and arrange the meat in the center of a platter, as shown.

⑤ Cut the legs crosswise into slices and arrange them on both sides of the platter.

⑥ Arrange the wings at the opposite end of the legs.

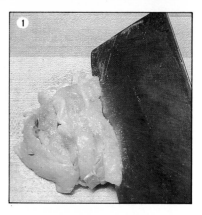

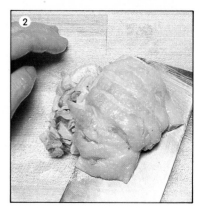

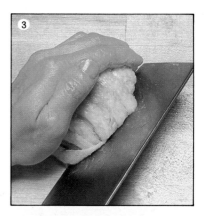

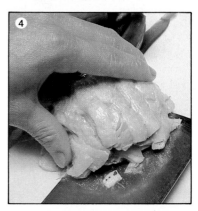

①將雞塊略修整齊，切下的邊角及較碎的肉先切小塊堆一邊。再將雞塊剁成
　長方塊。
②將整齊的肉塊蓋在碎塊上，並用手拱起成半圓形。
③用刀面剷起。
④放在大盤上。使用五種不同材料，照上法堆排成梅花形，在空隙擺些盤飾
　即成"五福拼盤"。

① Use a cooked (boiled) chicken breast for this platter. Trim the
chicken breast to obtain a neat bulk. Set aside the pieces of meat
that have been trimmed off. Cut the chicken breast into strips.
② Gather together the pieces of chicken breast that were trimmed off.
Use the flat side of a cleaver to carefully pick up the pieces of
chicken. Place the strips of chicken over the pieces that were
trimmed off. Use your hands to mold and pack the chicken
together.
③ Use the flat side of a cleaver to lift the packed chicken meat.
④ Carefully set it on a serving platter. An assortment of four other
ingredients are arranged on the platter to resemble a plum
blossom.

牛肉盤飾 • Cold Beef Platter

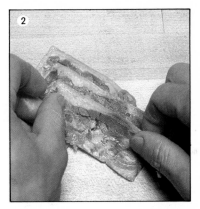

①將牛肉塊略修整齊，切下的邊角及較碎的肉先切片 堆一邊。

②將牛肉塊切長方片，左右交疊排好。

③兩邊修齊。

④用刀面劍起置碎肉堆上，連同碎肉一併劍起置於大盤上。使用七種不同材
料，照上法堆排成星形，中央放些核桃並配上盤飾即成"柒味大拼盤"。

① Use 1 lb. cooked beef shank for this platter. Trim the shank to obtain
a rectangular bulk. Set aside the pieces that have been trimmed off.

② Slice across the rectangular piece of beef. Arrange the slices to form
an inverted "v" by alternating sides.

③ Trim the two sides to obtain straight edges after the sliced beef has
been arranged.

④ Gather together the pieces that were trimmed off to form a neat
mound. Use the flat side of a cleaver to pick up the arranged sliced
beef; place it over the mound of beef. Use the flat side of a cleaver to
lift the beef arrangement and carefully set it on a serving platter. Use
five other ingredients to obtain a star design, as shown. Crispy fried
walnuts are used in the center of the star design in the illustration.

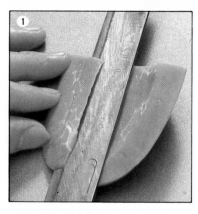

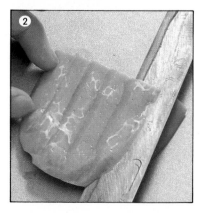

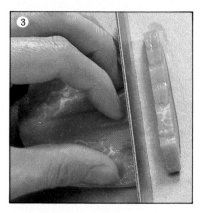

①處理乾淨泡水後的腰子，取⅟₄塊，在內面斜刀深切至¾處。

②連續斜切五或六刀。

③取橫的，切片，第一刀不切斷，第二刀切斷。

④由中央打開即成鳳尾狀。

　放入開水內燙熟，待顏色轉變立即撈出，浸入冷水內漂涼。使用時由切口
　處打開即現出其花樣。

① Use one-fourth of a pork kidney for this garnish. Turn the cutting knife so that the flat side is parallel to the cutting surface. Cut the kidney in half lengthwise. Remove the extraneous white matter from the middle of the kidney. Cut the halves in half crosswise. Place the kidney with the straight edge away from you. On the cut surface, diagonally make several cuts to one-fourth of the opposite edge.

② Continue to make five or six diagonal cuts as before.

③ Turn the piece of kidney so that the diagonal cuts are in a horizontal position. Slice the kidney across the diagonal cuts, do not cut through the first cut; cut through the second slice.

④ Carefully open the first two slices. The design will resemble the tail of a phoenix. Open the remaining slices.

Cook the pieces of kidney in boiling water until their color changes; remove. Plunge the pieces of kidney in cold water; remove. Open the kidney design and arrange the pieces on a platter, as illustrated.

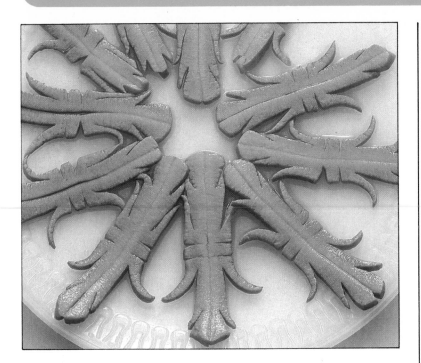

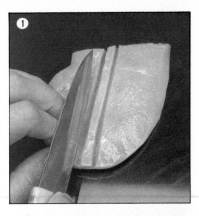

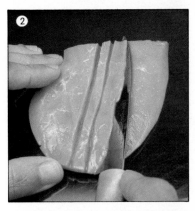

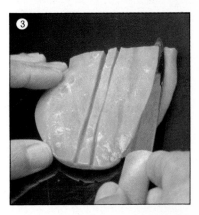

① 處理乾淨泡水後的腰子，取¼塊。在內面中央切兩直刀深至¾處。

② 靠右邊先斜切一刀。

③ 緊接着再斜切一刀。左邊亦同樣斜切兩刀。

④ 取橫的，切片，第一刀不切斷，第二刀切斷。
　放入開水內燙熟，待顏色轉變立即撈出，浸入冷水內漂涼。使用時由切口
　處打開即現出"壽"字圖案。

① Use one-fourth of a pork kidney for this garnish. Turn the cutting knife so that the flat side is parallel to the cutting surface. Cut the kidney in half lengthwise. Remove the extraneous white matter from the middle of the kidney. Cut the halves in half crosswise. Place the kidney with the straight edge away from you. On the cut surface, make two cuts in the center (vertically), as shown.

② Make one diagonal cut from the edge of the kidney down toward the two center cuts made in Step ① ; do not cut through.

③ Make a second cut under the first cut. Make two similar center cuts on the other side of the kidney.

④ Turn the kidney so that all previously made cuts are in a horizontal position. Slice the kidney, do not cut through the first cut; cut through the second slice.
Cook the pieces of kidney in boiling water until their color changes; remove. Plunge the pieces of kidney in cold water. Open the kidney design and arrange the pieces on a platter, as illustrated. The design is called "long life".

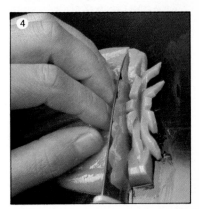

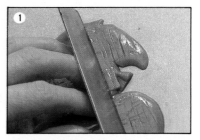

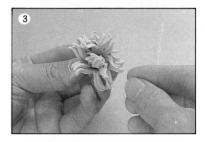

① 處理乾淨泡水後的腰子，橫切取半塊，在表面每隔 0.3公分劃直刀紋深至 $\frac{3}{4}$。

② 取橫的,斜刀片薄片。放入開水內燙熟,待顏色轉變立即撈出,浸入冷水內漂涼。

③ 取一片捲成花心。

④ 繼續一片片的包捲上,做成所要花朵的大小即可。

⑤⑥也可用墨魚來做,做法相同。

① Use one-half of a pork kidney for this garnish. Turn the cutting knife so that the flat side is parallel to the cutting surface. Cut the kidney in half lengthwise. Remove the extraneous white matter from the middle of the kidney. Make 1/8 inch cuts on three-fourths of the piece of kidney, do not cut through.

② Turn the piece of kidney so that the 1/8 inch cuts are in a horizontal position. Slant the cutting knife to a 30°angle; place it one inch from the edge of the kidney. Diagonally slice off one-inch pieces. Cook the pieces of kidney in boiling water until their color changes; remove. Plunge the pieces of kidney in cold water; remove.

③ Take one piece of cooked kidney and roll it like a jelly roll, starting at the boarder, to form the center of the flower.

④ Place the other pieces of kidney around the center petal until the flower design is completed.

⑤⑥ Squid may also used for this garnish.

①②皮蛋置檯上（或拿在手上），一邊切一邊不時的搖動刀子，才能切出波浪形花紋。

③先切半。

④同樣方法，每半個再切成三塊。

⑤皮蛋亦可切橫片，邊切邊搖動刀子，以切出花紋。

⑥切成 0.5 公分的薄片，一個蛋約可切出6—7片。

①② Place a one thousand year egg on a flat surface. Cut the egg in half lengthwise, move the knife slightly from side to side to produce a ripple effect. You may also hold the egg in your hand and cut the egg in half as directed above.

③ Separate the halves.

④ Cut each half, lengthwise, into three wedges. Arrange the egg wedges on a platter as illustrated, or as desired. OR

⑤ Cut the thousand year egg crosswise into 1/4 inch slices; move the knife slightly from side to side to produce a ripple effect.

⑥ An egg may be cut into six or seven slices.

蛋黃盤飾 • Egg Yolk Garnish

①將蛋黃取出放在容器內。
②加少許鹽打散。
③油燒熱，漏杓置鍋上方，炸時一邊搖動漏杓一邊將蛋液倒入漏杓內。
④待蛋黃浮起即撈出，蛋黃呈珠粒狀即成。

①Place five egg yolks in a bowl.
②Add salt, to taste, and beat lightly.
③Heat oil in a wok. Hold a wire sieve three inches above the oil; pour the beaten egg yolks into the sieve while moving the sieve from side to side.
④Remove the egg yolks from the hot oil as soon as they surface. The egg yolks will have formed into small balls.

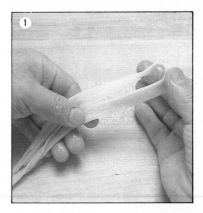

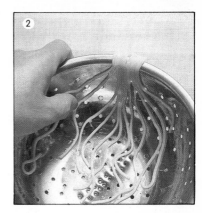

① 將麵條煮熟，用冷水沖涼，瀝乾水份，拌些油。用食指勾上 5 或 6 根麵條。
② 將麵條排在有洞的碗形容器內，手指勾出的環狀露在容器外，每組麵條的底端都需鋪散開，且依序相疊，炸出的籃子才會結實不變形。
③ 將麵條整齊緊密的排滿後，在有空隙的地方補些麵條。
④ 用另一個相同的容器蓋在上面，置油內炸後，即成花籃。

① Cook the spaghetti noodles as directed on package. Place the cooked noodles in water; drain. Add a little oil to the noodles and gently stir them. Fold five or six noodles, in half, over your index finger.

② Place the strands of noodles in a colander, as illustrated. The folded loop should be draped over the edge. Continue to place the folded noodles (5 to 6 to each group) around the colander, as shown. Separate the ends of the noodles that fall into the middle of the colander. The ends of the noodles should be intertwined to form a woven pattern. This will make the noodle basket stronger and the noodles will not separate during deep-frying.

③ Place the remaining noodles in the center of the colander or wherever needed to reinforce the center of the weave pattern.

④ Place another colander on top of the noodles, as illustrated. Set the colanders in a wok of hot oil. Use a ladle with a long handle to hold the top colander in place. Evenly deep-fry the noodles; remove the noodle basket; drain.

木須肉皮盤飾 • Moo Shu Skin Garnish

① 先將油略燒熱。在麵皮上戳洞備用。
② 麵皮放入油鍋內。
③ 用大瓢按住以固定形狀。
④ 炸酥後撈出。

① Use a fork to prick small holes through a moo shu skin.
② Place the moo shu skin in hot oil.
③ Place a laddle on top of the moo shu skin to hold it down in the oil and to give it a concave shape.
④ Remove the moo shu skin when it golden; drain.

馬鈴薯盤飾 • Potato Garnish

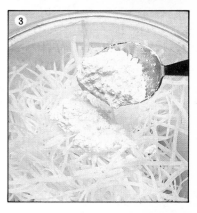

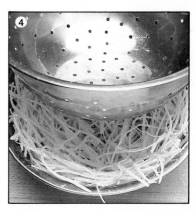

① 馬鈴薯切絲，浸泡在水裏約1小時，泡時換水二或三回。
② 取出瀝乾水份。
③ 拌入太白粉。
④ 將碗形容器內抹油，把馬鈴薯絲鋪滿在容器內，再用另一個相同的容器蓋上，置油鍋內炸熟，即成"雀巢"。

① Cut a potato into thin strips. Soak the potato strips in water for 1 hour; change the water several times during the hour.
② Drain the potato strips.
③ Lightly Sprinkle the potato strips with cornstarch to absorb dampness and to make the potato strips crispier.
④ Heat oil in a wok over medium heat. Dip the wire strainers in the oil to grease them lightly. Arrange the potato strips in the wire strainer; place another strainer on top of the potatoes. Submerge the strainers into the oil and deep-fry until the potatoes are golden. The garnish should resemble a bird's nest.

A Series of Books for Your Pleasure and Enjoyment

CHINESE CUISINE

- 180 recipes
- 204 pages
- Paperbound edition
- Chinese, Chinese/English (bilingual), English, Japanese and French editions

CHINESE COOKING FOR BEGINNERS

- 89 recipes and 10 snacks
- 104 pages
- Paperbound edition
- Chinese and English editions

CHINESE CUISINE II

- 187 recipes and 50 garnishes
- 280 pages
- Hardbound edition
- Chinese/English (bilingual) edition

CHINESE APPETIZERS AND GARNISHES

- 78 appetizers and 86 garnishes
- 164 pages
- Paperbound edition
- Chinese/English (bilingual) edition

CHINESE SNACKS

- 98 snacks
- 100 pages
- Paperbound edition
- Chinese/English (bilingual) edition

CHINESE SEAFOOD

- 127 recipes
- 108 pages
- Paperbound edition
- Chinese and English editions

MEDITATIONS ON NATURE

- 90 flower arrangement methods
- 184 pages
- Hardbound edition
- Chinese/English (bilingual) edition

These books are all 7¼"x10¼" and include full-color photographs. Each paperbound book is encased in a clear plastic cover.

 WEI-CHUAN'S COOK BOOKS